CODING FOR BEGINNERS:

A SIMPLIFIED GUIDE FOR BEGINNERS TO LEARN SELF-TAUGHT CODING STEP BY STEP. BECOME AN EXPERT CODER IN THE SHORTEST TIME POSSIBLE.

Eugene Gates

Coding for Beginners

© Copyright 2020 - All rights reserved.

The content contained within this book may not be reproduced, duplicated or transmitted without direct written permission from the author or the publisher.

Under no circumstances will any blame or legal responsibility be held against the publisher, or author, for any damages, reparation, or monetary loss due to the information contained within this book. Either directly or indirectly.

Legal Notice: This book is copyright protected. This book is only for personal use. You cannot amend, distribute, sell, use, quote or paraphrase any part, or the content within this book, without the consent of the author or publisher.

Disclaimer Notice: Please note the information contained within this document is for educational and entertainment purposes only. All effort has been executed to present accurate, up to date, and reliable, complete information. No warranties of any kind are declared or implied. Readers acknowledge that the author is not engaging in the rendering of legal, financial, medical or professional advice. The content within this book has been derived from various sources. Please consult a licensed professional before attempting any techniques outlined in this book.

By reading this document, the reader agrees that under no circumstances is the author responsible for any losses, direct or indirect, which are incurred as a result of the use of information contained within this document, including, but not limited to, — errors, omissions, or inaccuracies.

Table of Contents

Introduction 5

Chapter 1:   *Web Programming* *9*

Chapter 2:   *Getting Started With Coding* 17

Chapter 3:   *Functions* 23

Chapter 4:   *Containers* 33

Chapter 5:   *Strings* 35

Chapter 6:   *Loops* 45

Chapter 7:   *Modules* 59

Chapter 8:   *Files* 67

Chapter 9:   *Programming Paradigms* 77

Chapter 10:   *Object-Oriented Programming* 79

Chapter 11:   *Misconceptions About Coding* *89*

Chapter 12:   *Bash* *95*

Chapter 13:   *Regular Expressions* 103

Chapter 14:   *Data Structures* 113

Chapter 15:   *Algorithms* 123

Chapter 16:   *Logical Switches* 127

Chapter 17:   *Coding Practices* 131

Chapter 18:   *How to Be an Expert Coder in the Shortest Time Possible* 137

Chapter 19:   *Other Factors* 143

Chapter 20:   *Landing a Job* 149

Coding for Beginners

Conclusion..155

Introduction

Computers are a lot different from humans.

They are not neutrally active and doesn't consist of any emotions that humans possess. Computers mostly rely on instructions.

The only reason why computers have become better than humans is that they do tasks effectively without wasting any time. However, we can consider computers as dumb machines. If they are not provided with a solution to the problem beforehand, they can't solve it. Even after twenty years of tremendous research robotics is not a successful field because it is challenging to make machines that take decisions by themselves.

In the early stages of computer development, people used to use instruction sets to complete tasks. These instructions sets are allowed to use only for scientific and military purposes.

Several multinational companies started to experiment with their employees to create a whole new way to pass instructions to computers. All dreamt of an easy way to make things work out.

After a few years with excellent research, computer scientists introduced the concept of programming to the technological world with the help of programming languages. Programming languages provide a set of defined libraries that can help you to create programs.

Programs are considered as an analytical representation of algorithms and the definite task of creating valid programs that can be understood by a machine is known as programming.

What is a Program?

Programming languages use programs to give varied instructions to the computing machines. From a mathematical perspective, the process of providing step-by-step instructions is called an algorithm.

Coding for Beginners

A lot of statistical concepts in mathematics too use algorithms to solve a problem. An algorithm is not only a step-by-step procedure but a way that is proven to be effective.

In programming, we use programs to create a logical instruction that can make us solve a specific problem as quickly and effectively as possible.

Experienced programmers try to create programs that are in less code length and which consumes fewer resources. It is not only essential to create a working code, but it is also important to develop code that is feasible and which effectively understands the resources that are available to it.

What is the difference between Algorithm & program?

Algorithm and program are closely interlinked. When a programmer is solving a problem, he first finds a logical and provable way to complete it.

He monitors the inputs and outputs that are available and creates a step-by-step procedure to solve it.

This is called an algorithm from a theoretical basis.

However, computers can't understand human language. They use the binary system to follow instructions.

This is the reason why we need to represent our algorithm in a way such that computers can understand.

This process is technically known as programming. Programming uses a set of programs to make the computer understand what needs to be done.

What are the programming languages?

When the concept of programming is introduced the scientific and computing community has overwhelmed. They started developing a lot of instruction sets and began developing programs with them.

However, just after a few projects programmers and computing scientists understood that there needs to be a specific regular platform to create programs. It is not feasible to use each other's instruction sets to create meaningful software.

So, they worked hard to develop programming languages that can maintain and provide a lot of libraries for their usage. Programming languages like ABC, Pascal are developed and people started using them for developing programs. All these distinct programming libraries are enhanced and named as programming languages. They are also called as high-level languages and remember that they are only used to make it easy for humans to communicate with computers.

We always need a compiler to let computers understand the program.

To understand C programming in depth it is vital to learn about the default programming process in detail. Just like every other technological advancement, programming languages too follow a strictly adhered guideline system to make things work in the way they are intended to.

As said before, it is difficult to make computers understand the programs by themselves. So, computer scientists started to create programs that can be compiled and converted into machine language.

All the programs are compiled, interpreted before running the program.

This task is done by interpreters and compilers.

Coding for Beginners

Chapter 1: Web Programming

Web programming, also referred to as web development, is an elaborate process where programmers build dynamic applications for use on the internet. Some of the popular web applications today include business platforms like Amazon and social networks like Facebook and Twitter.

While these are some of the top names in the industry, it is easy to assume that web programming is hard. It takes a lot of practice, but in essence web development is one of the easiest forms of coding you can learn as a programmer. When writing code for a website, you see immediate results, which help you determine whether you are doing the right thing, or need to ask for help. Besides, today there are so many tools and resources available online that you can use to learn.

There are two categories of web development; front-end development and back-end development. Front-end development is also known as client-side development. It involves building the side of the application that the user interacts with whenever they load the application. This includes the design and content, and how the user interacts with the application. Front-end development is primarily written in JavaScript, CSS and HTML.

Back-end development, also referred to as server-side development deals with everything else that takes place behind the scenes. Users do not see this, but it is the engine that powers what they interact with whenever they are online. You need a database for the back-end, which will eventually power the front-end. There are many programming languages that can be used to build the server-side, including Java, Python, PHP, and Perl.

Factors to consider when choosing a programming language

Given that there are so many languages available, it might not be easy for you to choose one for your project. There are some factors, however, that can guide your choice, and help make your work easier, as follows:

- **Tool support**

Coding for Beginners

You should always consider working with a programming language that has all the tools you need to build your project effortlessly. This way, you will not just manage to build the application, but you can also maintain it without a hitch.

- **Size of the project**

The sheer size of some projects necessitates the use of specific languages. Some languages might be effective, but their performance is inhibited when the project scales up in size. A lot of startup companies realize this some years down the line. Once the business needs and application resource consumption grows, they have to switch to a different language.

- **Library support**

Before you settle on a given language, make sure you consider the library constraints. Ensure that the library available will not just meet your needs, but will also solve other needs arising down the line.

- **Elasticity**

Flexibility is one of the key features you must look at. For your projects, ensure you use a language that allows you to scale the application accordingly over time. This means you should manage to add or remove some features and programs into the application without affecting the performance.

- **Platform choice**

Always think about the platform upon which the application will run. While most languages support different platforms, their suitability might not be pleasant across the board. Take programs written in C, for example. These programs are best suited for Linux and Windows-based systems. While you might experiment with other platforms, the performance might not be as you would experience in a Windows or Linux environment.

Programming languages

If you are a beginner in web programming or software development, you might have come across so many languages to the point where you are unsure where to start. A lot of people have been there. There are so many languages to choose from. However, you need to know where to begin, and how to build on what you have learned. Here are some of the top programming languages in use today.

Python

Python stands out today as one of the most versatile programming languages in the world. When using Python, you can write code and at the same time run it without using a compiler. Python further boasts support for code readability. What this means is that its syntax structure allows you to write a few lines of code to make a point. This is also possible in C++ and Java. The interesting thing about Python is that while it is an advanced language, it is very easy, and beginner programmers can pick up on it very fast.

There are so many popular applications currently running on Python, including Google, Yahoo, Pinterest and Instagram. Most of these are websites and applications that are heavy on memory usage, which means that Python is not just perfect for automated memory management, it also features a very big library and supports various paradigms in development.

CSS

Cascading Style Sheets, CSS, is a markup language. It defines the way a website or web page appears, when coupled with HTML. Some of the elements that make up CSS determine things like the font style and size, colors and any other design features of the website.

CSS helps developers create visually pleasing websites. It has also come in handy in the development of appealing mobile applications too. CSS features a language syntax that is almost similar to XHTML and HTML. As a result, the language syntaxes can work together without a hitch.

Coding for Beginners

Java

Java is one of the most in-demand languages today. It is widely used in developing mobile apps and games. It is object-oriented, and is favored by most developers because it can be used across different platforms. Therefore, a program written on a Windows-based machine can still run on a Mac OS device.

JavaScript

JavaScript is currently one of the best programing languages you need to learn. It empowers you to manage the browser, allow front-end scripts to run, edit and display content on the website and so forth. JavaScript allows for asynchronous interaction between users and the application.

JavaScript is one of the most popular languages given its prevalence in game development and building desktop applications. All the major browsers support JavaScript, so you do not need plug-ins or a compiler to run an application.

JavaScript is a functional language. Objects in JavaScript are first-class, associating with their characteristics and functions. An example is a nested function, which is a function inside a function.

This is also one of the most dynamic languages because types are related to values, not variables. As a result, you can test project types in several ways. JavaScript is an object-oriented language, and as such all the objects within its environment are associative arrays.

PHP

Hypertext Processor, PHP, is a server-side language which is recommended for use in web development and other regular programming needs. PHP has been around since 2004, but currently powers hundreds of millions of websites all over the world.

Given that PHP is an interpreted script language, it is ideal for back-end programming because of the need for an interpreter. It is suitable for this type of programming because you can run server services in the background while still developing the application or website.

Ruby

Ruby is a dynamic programming language that has been around since 1993. Ruby is ideal for building websites and mobile applications. As a highly scalable language, it provides an astute balance between functional programming and imperative programming.

Ruby is not just easy to understand, it is also one of the easiest languages to write. However, for beginner developers who are just getting into Ruby, it is wise to start with Ruby on Rails. Ruby on Rails makes it easier for you to work with Ruby, and enjoy the experience.

Ruby is often recommended for websites or web servers that encounter lots of traffic. Some popular examples include Twitter and Hulu.

SQL

Structured Query Language, commonly identified in its abbreviated form SQL is a programming language that was specifically written for database operations. Data manipulation, storage and retrieval are some of the key features in SQL. A lot of web based frameworks run SQL today, given that it is effective in maintaining database integrity, is secure and maintains data precision.

C

C is similar to C++. It is a general purpose language that is often used to build supporting elements for other languages like Java, C++ and Python. This means that most of the supported languages borrow some features from C, such as standard libraries, syntax and control structures. This explains why it is always advisable that you learn C++ and C before you expand your knowledge to other languages, so that you have a firm foundation in the basics.

Coding for Beginners

C-Sharp (C#)

Microsoft developed C# in 2000 as an object-oriented programming language. It is popular in desktop applications, and became an integral part of applications built for Windows 8 and Windows 10. To run C# therefore, you must have the .NET framework installed on your computer. C# was built to compete with Java.

Compared with C++, C# has logical and consistent code, which is one of the reasons why it is one of the best languages for beginners to grasp. C# is a statically typed language, which means that you can check your code before you run it into applications. Therefore, it is easier to identify errors when programming in C#.

C++

C++ is a case-sensitive programming language. It is general purpose, and presents programmers with the necessary tools for memory manipulation at a low level. C++ is an interesting language because it combines the features of high-level languages and low-level languages. As a result, it is often construed as a mid-level language.

Primarily, C++ is an object-oriented language, thanks to the following inherent features:

- Data hiding
- Inheritance
- Encapsulation
- Polymorphism

C++ is a superset of C, so they share a lot of similarities. This also means that if you write a program in C, it is also a C++ program. C++ is a very detailed language. For beginners, it is advisable that you focus on the concepts instead of the details, lest you get confused.

So, where does this leave you? The best place for you to start depends on what you want to pursue in your career. If you feel database management is right for you, you should start with C++ or C to become an SQL developer.

Back-end developers will find JavaScript, PHP, Python, C#, Ruby and Python handy, while front-end developers should be okay with JavaScript.

If you plan to delve into game development, focus on C# and C++. Mobile app developers should emphasize Java, Swift and C#. Programmers who are interested in building desktop applications should focus on Python, C++ and Java.

Remember that this is one of the most dynamic industries. Therefore, expect new releases and updates from time to time. It is difficult to advise anyone which programming language is best because choices depend on needs assessment.

Coding for Beginners

Chapter 2: Getting Started With Coding

Preparing Your Vision

Think about why you wanted to learn to code in the first place. For a lot of people, it is because they want to make something that just doesn't exist yet. Others may want to do it because they know software developers are high-paying jobs and happen to be high in demand by tech and non-tech companies alike. Identify what drives you and then start looking for sources of inspiration that encourage you to stay focused on your goals. For a coder, an inspiration would be something like working for Apple or building the next competitor of Twitter. Identifying your vision is necessary in steering you towards the right tools. Like if you want to get involved with artificial intelligence and tinker with robots, Python is a functional starting language and has a lot of flexibility. If you're going to build the next Candy Crush addiction, you will need to focus on mobile apps and learn Swift, Objective-C, Kotlin and Java.

Preparing Your Program Structure

Building algorithms and flowcharts is essential. It is not an absolute requirement of course and you may be able to get away with making a quick piece of software without spending so much time on the planning phase but for the sake of efficiency and not wasting so much time taking multiple trips back to the drawing board, you should come up with a solid structure of your program. Rushing directly to the code editor without a plan would be like trying to build a house without a blueprint. Algorithms and flowcharts do not have to be a single night affair; you should take the time to study them and identify potential pain points or areas that may cause conflict. Depending on the size of your vision, a single mind may not be enough to run through all sorts of case scenarios. Let other people or perhaps friends take a look at your flowchart and algorithm so you can get their user perspectives. If you don't feel like the structure lacks polish,

Coding for Beginners

don't rush things because realizing there is a problem during the coding phase can cause a world of issues.

Preparing Your Hardware

The really cool thing about coding is the hard fact that you don't need a fancy computer to get started. Even an ancient Windows XP laptop can be capable of coding as long as you install the right software. Of course, your mileage will be significantly reduced with low-end hardware so I'm going to recommend something a bit more middle ground while keeping things budget-friendly. Coding is not by any means a huge investment! Your choice of hardware depends on where you will spend time coding for the most part.

If You Are A Home And/Or Office Dweller

Desktop computers remain as the best bang-for-the-buck coding workstations and it's pretty easy to explain why. Mobile components and chipsets tend to be more expensive and today's powerful laptops are very thin with sophisticated engineering. They also have parts that you don't find in desktops like trackpads, keyboards and batteries. Performance absolutely matters when you are compiling a program, using an interpreter or debugger, running a complicated program.

So what's the best processor to choose? Or more specifically, what's the best combination of desktop specs to consider? The answer is straightforward when it comes to coding and you don't even have to worry about the brand. For the CPU choice, the more cores, the better. The higher the clock speed (in GHz), the better. If you are stuck picking between Intel and AMD, go with the one with the lower price. If you have Windows 10, you should at least have 8 GB of RAM or else coding might not be so fun since Windows 10 tends to eat a significant chunk of your RAM with nothing running and you will probably need a browser tab or two open followed by whatever IDE or source-code editor you plan on using. More RAM means your system is less likely to bog down when you have lots of applications running at the same time.

The next key component of a coding workstation is the monitor. A modern computer screen has a screen resolution of 1366×768. You can see what that looks like below at 100% scaling.

It doesn't look too bad. With a font size of 11, you can see about 27 lines of code on a maximized screen and there is a little bit of space for a sidebar or side panel which you can find in many IDEs and coding environments. EmEditor is more on the source code editing side and is suitable for beginners but when you factor in things like testing code, you are going to wish you had a little bit more screen real estate. Having a Full HD display or 1920×1080 resolution is a significant upgrade and pretty inexpensive thanks to the advent of 4K displays. But could you go beyond 1080p? Would 4K be a wise choice? If you are a beginner, 4K is a waste unless you plan on using font scaling which will make the characters a whole lot smoother. The real winner is to use multiple displays.

A pair of 1080p displays will make a world of difference even if you are a beginner programmer. It is much better than those ultrawide displays that spreadsheet fanatics love. You do not need

Coding for Beginners

an ultrawide display since coders generally need more vertical screen real estate. But with a two displays and set in "extended desktop" mode, you can have a full screen dedicated to your coding environment and another screen for another coding environment if you like doing multiple projects or managing different codes or you can open up your browser for research or your flowchart or anything you just want to drag there at your leisure.

Next up is the keyboard and this is going to surprise you if you've been stuck with the same $10-$20 keyboard for the past several years. You might even be pretty comfortable mashing away at 60-70 words per minute and not thinking about "fixing what isn't broken". Try a mechanical keyboard as soon as you have the budget.

If You Are A Road Warrior

Picking a laptop geared towards coding is going to be a little bit more complicated since virtually all laptops come with each of their own compromises. It's really going to boil down to preference and what strengths of a computer you really need and even then you might still have a lot of laptops to choose from. But with this, should be able to narrow down your selection to the point that all the remaining candidates are winners. Prepare your checklist!

You obviously want to address the portability first as that should be the reason why you want to consider a laptop in the first place. A heavier laptop often means heavy-duty while a lighter laptop means more travel-friendly at the expense of flexibility in terms of handling coding and programming apps.

No matter what type of laptop you are going to get, having 8 GB worth of RAM along with an SSD and a 1080p display should be the three core essentials to consider. If you are really on a shoestring budget, the 1080p display should be your minimum. Then make sure you can upgrade your RAM and storage as there are several budget thin and light laptops that have soldered parts and are therefore non-upgradable.

Preparing Your Software

Flowcharting Software

Drawing a flowchart is easy but if you want to present a pretty complicated program flow in the cleanest way possible or just want to sort out your thoughts and algorithm in a friendly way, you should use a flowcharting software. If you have an active Internet connection, then I have some good news; you don't have to install any flowcharting software at all! Just head to http://www.draw.io and you can immediately get started with illustrating. Draw.io has a gridded interface and is pretty easy to learn as the flowcharting shapes are readily available on the sidebar. Connecting the shapes with arrows is pretty straightforward. You can save your work on Google Drive, OneDrive, Dropbox and a few code repositories or you can save it right on your computer. There is even an "Offline" option so you can switch off your Internet without fear of the web-based app interrupting your workflow.

Web Development Tools

C++ is a great programming language to play around with for understanding the basics of coding but if you want to go hands-on the fastest way possible, give HTML a shot because there is a useful and free (with ads) sandbox for placing HTML codes called https://htmlcodeeditor.com . The user interface isn't exquisite but it has a live preview so you can play around with the different codes and see the end result in real-time. You don't have to wait for anything to compile even though you are restricted to pure classic HTML code. CSS support is only available in the paid version.

If you want a free solution you can install to your Windows computer, give openElement a try. This Chromium-powered Web authoring tool has been around for several years and it is ready for the modern Web development world with support for HTML5 and CSS3. It even comes with a local server so you can test PHP scripts.

Coding for Beginners

Source Code Editors

Whether you are going to take the nomadic route and do some pure raw coding or you are going to try out fancy IDEs, it always helps to have at least one source code editor installed in your computer. Source code editors are generally not heavy apps by any stretch and beginners have no reason to go for any paid software over the free ones. Just install Notepad++ and you'll see exactly what I mean. In addition to full HTML support for syntax highlighting, Notepad++ supports more than a dozen other programming languages. For a more elegant but still free alternative, you should try Sublime Text and it has Mac and Linux versions too in addition to Windows. The dark-themed interface should blend well with your dark mode themes and it has a highly customizable user interface.

IDEs

Once you are ready to move on beyond HTML, Python should be your next stop as it is one of the most accessible modern programming languages to learn. To quickly get started, consider trying PyCharm which is an IDE that even the pros use. The smart assistance feature helps with the debugging while the extensive documentation can walk you through the different features so you can run and test web apps. JavaScript, TypeScript, CoffeeScript, HTML, CSS and other technologies are supported by this IDE. If you want to expand beyond HTML and CSS and dive into JavaScript, Java and PHP, install Apache NetBeans IDE. Google even has its own IDE called Android Studio serving as the primary IDE for developing Android mobile apps with Kotlin as the primary language.

Chapter 3: Functions

Remember how we asked Merlin to store a set of commands in a file and later referenced that file whenever we wanted to repeat the same exact commands?

Well, we basically used what we'll call from now on, "functions". A function is effectively a block of statements that takes in inputs from other parts in the program, processes (or doesn't, in some cases) these inputs, and gives results.

So, an entire program can contain multiple functions and these functions can be invoked multiple times depending on what use we have for them. Why do we need functions though?

Well, primarily because we will need them sometimes. We will be dealing with really complex problems where we will end up using functions in order to write reusable code. Sometimes, problems are so big that we have to break our approach to solving them into steps and we can model each such step using a function. It is a very effective way of organizing both code and our thoughts.

Quick question - what function have you already seen in C++? The main function! It is a particular type of function that defines all the code that will run.

Let's see how we can define a function and run a function in C++:

```cpp
#include<iostream>

using namespace std;

int sum(int a, int b) {

int returnSum = a + b;

return returnSum;

}
```

Coding for Beginners

```
int main() {

int numOne = 10;

int numTwo = 20;




int sumValue = sum(numOne, numTwo);

//sumValue will have the value 30

cout << sumValue;

}
```

The above program creates and uses a function called sum, to compute the amount of two numbers and return the result. Usually, you wouldn't make functions for

such trivial applications but we're looking at the above program to learn about functions.

Let's look at the function call first -

```
int sumValue = sum(numOne, numTwo);
```

The above statement calls the function by passing in the variables numOne and numTwo to be processed by the sum function (definition is mentioned above the main function) and the result of the computation done by the function is then assigned to the variable sumValue.

Let's look at the function definition:

```
int sum(int a, int b) {

int returnSum = a + b;
```

return returnSum;

}

The variables in the parentheses (a and b) specify the datatype and labels for the variables that will be sent to the function. Once returnSum is computed, we use the "return" keyword to specify that we want this value to be sent to back to wherever the function is being called once the necessary computation/processing/work is done. Note that the variables a and b hold the values that are sent to the function. Also, the reason the value of the variable

returnSum will be accessible outside the function is that its value is being sent out of the function. If you created any other variable for any other purposes inside the function it wouldn't be accessible outside the function. In other words, it's "scope" is limited to the function in which it is defined.

The function itself has a datatype. This data type specifies the data type of the value being returned. So, if your function returns a string its value is eventually being stored in a variable with a double datatype, C++ would raise an error. It would first try to make sense of your mistake and try to convert the string to a double but because such a conversion is not possible, it would then raise an error.

Let's look at another example of a function -

```cpp
#include<iostream>

using namespace std;

void functionExample() {

cout << "This function does nothing!" << endl;

}

int main() {

functionExample();
```

Coding for Beginners

```
}
```

In the above function, we've defined a function called functionExample. Pay attention to the syntax. The function's data type is "void" which is a keyword that indicates that the function does not return a result to from where it was called.

The statements within the curly braces following the function name specify what the function does. In order to utilize the function, you will have to use it in other functions by specifying its name and passing variables. For example, in the above program, the function is called from the primary function by the command

"functionExample();".

Pass By Value and Pass By Reference:

Remember how we passed variables to our functions? That's a widespread thing to do in any language that you will come across. However, C++ has a unique feature when it comes to this particular process.

Let's look at what this is through an example -

```
#include<iostream>
#include<string>
using namespace std;
void addTwo(int input) {
input = input + 2;
}
int main() {
int a = 10;
```

```cpp
addTwo(a);

cout << a << endl;

}
```

The program above adds 2 to whatever the input value is. One would usually expect that the output of the program would be a 12. But, it is actually a 10. This is because even though the value 10 and the variable a is passed to the function addTwo, it's value is copied to the input variable in addTwo. As a result, C++

treats the variables a and input as two separate entities even though they share the same value. The variable input effectively copies the value of the variable a.

Pass By Reference:

In order to modify this behavior, we'll make use of the ampersand operator (&) just before mentioning the label for the inputVariable. This would make C++ look

at the inputVariable's label as an alias for the variable that's being passed in. Any modifications made to this "alias" would now also affect the variable whose value was passed in. This way of passing a variable to a function is termed as passing by reference. Let's modify the function we just worked with -

```cpp
#include<iostream>

#include<string>

using namespace std;

void addTwo(int& input) {

input = input + 2;

}

int main() {
```

Coding for Beginners

```cpp
int a = 10;

addTwo(a);

cout << a << endl;

}
```

The output would be 12.

Example - Write a program that reverses any string that the user provides.

```cpp
#include<iostream>

#include<string>

using namespace std;

string reverseString(string input) {

string reverse = "";

for (int counter = input.size() - 1;counter >= 0;counter--) {

reverse = reverse + input[counter];

}

return reverse;

}

int main() {

string str;

cout << "Enter a string: ";
```

cin >> str;

string reversedString = reverseString(str);

cout << "Reversed String: "<<reversedString<<endl; cout << "Original String: " << str << endl;

}

Example Output:

Enter a string: Library

Reversed String: yrarbiL

Original String: Library

Press any key to continue . . .

The above program takes in a string and passes it to the reverseString function which traverses the string from the last letter and adds it to an empty string until it reaches the index 0. The function then returns this newly formed string. Since we are passing by value the value of the original string (str) does not change.

Example- Check if a given string is a palindrome. Assume that every string that is sent in as input is always in lowercase. (Hint - a palindrome when reversed still matches the original string)

```
#include<iostream>
#include<string>
using namespace std; string reverseString(string input) {
string reverse = "";
for (int counter = input.size() - 1;counter >= 0;counter--) {
reverse = reverse + input[counter];
```

Coding for Beginners

```cpp
}

return reverse;

}

bool isPalindrome(string input) {

string reverse = reverseString(input);

if (reverse == input) {

return true;

}

else {

return false;

}

}

int main() {

string str;

cout << "Enter a string: ";

cin >> str;

string reversedString = reverseString(str);

cout << "Reversed String: "<<reversedString<<endl; cout << "Original String: " << str <<
endl; if (isPalindrome(str)) {

cout << "The string you entered is a palindrome." << endl;
```

```
}

else {

cout << "The string you entered is not a palindrome" << endl;

}

}
```

In the above program, the isPalindrome function calls the reverse function and uses the reverse of the input string to determine whether the string is a palindrome or not. Notice how the function call (isPalindrome()) has been used in an if-else block as it returns a bool value. This program can be simplified and written better but it has been written in this way to show how it can be built from the former program by just adding another function.

Example Outputs -

1)

Enter a string: madam

Reversed String: madam

Original String: madam

The string you entered is a palindrome.

Press any key to continue . . .

2)

Enter a string: palindrome

Reversed String: emordnilap

Original String: palindrome

The string you entered is not a palindrome

Coding for Beginners

Press any key to continue . . .

Eugene Gates

Chapter 4: Containers

Containers are precisely what their name conveys. They hold data in forms that are easily accessible for us. We will look at arrays and vectors.

Arrays:

Arrays are containers that hold data of a particular data type and are fixed in size. That is, once you initialize an array with a specific size you can't increase its size unless you create another variety of a larger size and copy over all the elements. Arrays also hold data in a linear sequence and preserve "order". Once data is put inside an array, it stays in the exact place you put it in unless you make changes to the variety.

Arrays are also not for beginner coders but when used properly, you can make far more efficient programs. If you find yourself making too many variables to store similar data, you can simplify things by creating an array that can store these values in their own dedicated cells. Think about the way apartments and condos work. Each room doesn't have its private mailbox. Instead, there is a dedicated room in the apartment containing a large mailbox with individual compartments each with their own locks to represent each room.

Let's learn how to create an array through an example:

```
#include<iostream>

using namespace std;

int main() {

int arrayOfNumbers[5] = { 10,23,45,67,12 };

}
```

The above example shows how to create an array. The array is defined by the label "arrayOfNumbers". The number within the square braces - 5 in this case establishes the number

Coding for Beginners

of elements the array holds. The "int" specifies that the array will contain only integers. This datatype can be changed depending on what type of array you want to create. Finally, the numbers within the curly braces represent the data that the array holds. When you initialize an array with its values, you specify the values between the curly braces.

To access a number, say 23, within the array, we do so by specifying an "index"

as follows -

cout<<arrayOfNumbers[1];

The above statement will print the number 23 on to the screen. Now you may notice I used the number 1 as my index and not 2. That's because C++ follows zero-based numbering where the first number in a collection starts at the index 0. So, in order to access the first number in arrayOfNumbers, you would use the 0 index like -

cout<<arrayOfNumbers[0];

Instead of initializing the array at the very moment you declare it, you can create it and later assign individual values to each position by indexing it. By the same logic, you can modify the values in the array as well.

So, you can do things like -

arrayOfNumbers[1] = arrayOfNumbers[1] + arrayOfNumbers[2] - 5; Now, arrayOfNumbers[1] would equal 63.

Everything looks fine and dandy until now doesn't it? Well, what would you do if your array had 200 elements and you had to go through each component and add 5 to it? You can't do something like arrayOfNumbers + 5, because arrayOfNumbers is a "container" that holds numbers. It points to a memory space in your computer that contains the numbers in the array. So, adding 5 to arrayOfNumbers doesn't make sense and will actually throw an error.

Chapter 5: Strings

String refers to the group of words which can be of meaningful or without meaning.

String basically used to represent text and characters in programming language. It always carry multiple characters to named as string. In other words strings are array but of character datatype. An array of character is called string. Strings are one dimensional array of character which areASCII terminated by null character represented by '\0'. A-Z = 65-90 a- z = 97-122 0-9 = 48-57

Example: Physical representation of
 string of size 6 which conations string "Hello" in computer memory.

Address in computer memory

600 601 602 603 604 605 H e l l o \0 A[0] A[1] A[2] A[3] A[4] A[5]

Name of array

Function of Strings

There are basically four functions in String
 1. Strlen()
 2. Strcpy()
 3. Strcat()
 4. Strcmp()

strlen() :

This function is used to find the length of a String.

For example :-
 Char str[5] = {"Hello"};
 int l ;
 l = Strlen(str);

Coding for Beginners

strcpy() : This function is used to copy String from one string variable to another string variable.

For ex :-
```
Char str[5] = {"Hello"} , str2[6] = {"World"} ; //Strcpy(destination , source);
Strcpy(str , str2);
```

strcat() :

This function is used to concat two string or to join two strings variable .

For ex :-
```
Char str[5] = {"Hello"} , str2[6] = {"World"} ; //Strcat(destination , source);
Strcpy(str , str2);
```

strcmp() :

This function is used to compare two string or to join two string variable.

For ex :-
```
Char str[5] = {"Hello"} , str2[6] = {"World"} ; //if (Strcmp (str , str2)==0)
Then both string variable are same
//if (Strcmp (str,str2)>0)
Then str is greater
//if (Strcmp (str,str2)<0)
Then str2 is greater
```

Chapter Programs

1. A Program to read and display string without any space

```
#include<stdio.h>
#include<conio.h>
#include<string.h>
```

```c
void main()
{
char str [30];
clrcsr ();
printf ("\n Enter String : ");
scanf ("%s",str);
printf ("\n You typed = %s ",str); getch();
}
```

2 .A program to read and display string with space

```c
#include<stdio.h>
#include<conio.h>
#include<string.h>
void main()
{
char str [30];
clrcsr ();
printf ("\n Enter String : "); gets(str);
printf ("\n You typed = %s ",str); getch();
}
```

3. A program to find the length of the String

```c
#include<stdio.h>
#include<conio.h>
#include<string.h>
void main()
{
char str [30] , l;
clrcsr ();
printf ("\n Enter String : ");
```

Coding for Beginners

```
gets(str);
l = Strlen(str);

printf("\n Length of String %s is %d ", str ,l );
getch();
}
```

4. A program to read two string variables and concat or join them

```
#include<stdio.h>
#include<conio.h>
#include<string.h>
void main()
{
char str [30] , str1[30] ;
clrcsr ();
printf ("\n Enter 1st String : "); scanf ("%s",str);
printf ("\n Enter 2nd String : "); scanf("%d",str1);
strcat( str , str1);

Printf("\n Result after concatenation : %s ",str);
getch();
}
```

5. A program to copy a word from one string variable to another variable

```
#include<stdio.h>
#include<conio.h>
#include<string.h>
void main()
```

```c
{
char str [30] , str1[30] ;
clrcsr ();
printf ("\n Enter 1st String : ");
scanf ("%s",str);
printf("\n Enter 2nd String : ");
scanf("%d",str1);
strcpy( str , str1);
Printf("\n Result after copying : %s ",str); getch();
}
```

6. A program to check which string variable is greater

```c
#include<stdio.h>
#include<conio.h>
#include<string.h>
void main()
{
char str [30] , str1[30] ;
clrcsr();
printf ("\n Enter 1st String : "); scanf ("%s",str);
printf("\n Enter 2nd String : "); scanf("%d",str1);
if(strcmp (str , str1)>0)
{
printf("\n %s is greater ",str); else
{
printf("\n %s is greater ",str1); }
getch();
```

7. A program to count the number of alphabet 'a' in a sentence

Coding for Beginners

```c
#include<stdio.h>
#include<conio.h>
#include<string.h>
void main()
{
char str [30] ;
int count=0 , l , i ;
clrcsr ();
printf ("\n Write a sentence : "); scanf ("%s",str);
l = strlen(str);
for(i=0 ; i<l ; i++)
{
If( str[i] == 'a')

printf("\n Number of 'a' character in a sentence is : %d ",count);
getch();
}
```

8. A program to count the number of vowels in a sentence

```c
#include<stdio.h>
#include<conio.h>
#include<string.h>
char str [30] ;
int count=0 , l , i ;
clrcsr ();
printf ("\n Write a sentence : ");
scanf ("%s",str);
l = strlen(str);
```

```c
for(i=0 ; i<l ; i++)
{
If( str[i] == 'a' || str[i] == 'e' str[i] == 'i' || str[i] == 'o' || str[i] == 'u')

printf("\n Number of vowels in a sentence is : %d ",count);
getch();
}
```

9. A program to count the number of consonant in a sentence

```c
#include<stdio.h>
#include<conio.h>
#include<string.h>
char str [30] ;
int count=0 , l , i ;
clrcsr ();
printf ("\n Write a sentence : ");
scanf ("%s",str);
l = strlen(str);
for(i=0 ; i<l ; i++)
{
If( str[i] != 'a' || str[i] != 'e' str[i] != 'i' || str[i] !='o' || str[i] != 'u')
printf("\n Number of consonant in a sentence is : %d ",count);

getch();
}
```

10. A program to reverse a string

```c
#include<stdio.h>
#include<conio.h>
#include<string.h>
```

Coding for Beginners

```c
void main()
{
char str [30];
clrcsr ();
printf ("\n Enter String : ");
scanf ("%s",str);
strrev(str);
printf ("\n Reverse string = %s ",str); getch();
}
```

11. A program to change the string in both upper and lower case

```c
#include<stdio.h>
#include<conio.h>
#include<string.h>
void main()
{
char str [30] , str1[30];
clrcsr();
printf ("\n String in lower case : "); gets(str);
printf ("\n String in upper case : "); gets(str1);
strupr(str);
strlwr(str1);
printf("\n Lower to upper case %s",str); printf("\n Upper to lower case %s",str1); getch() ;
}
```

12. A program to compare two string variables without case comparing

```c
#include<stdio.h>
#include<conio.h>
#include<string.h>
```

```c
void main()
{
char str [30] , str1[30];
clrcsr();
printf ("\n Enter 1st word : ");
gets(str);
printf ("\n Enter 2nd word : "); gets(str1);
if( strcmpi (str , str1)==0) {
printf("\n Same ");
}
Else
{
printf("\n Not Same ");
}
getch();
```

Coding for Beginners

Chapter 6: Loops

Loops are a way for us to execute a set of statements multiple times. We can specify the number of times we want to accomplish these statements or we can also specify conditions which when are or are not satisfied with the execution of this set of statements stop.

There are three types of loops we're going to look at - for, while, do while Let's look at the for loop first -

The for loop is mostly used for executing a set of statements a set number of times. It's also used to iterate through extensive collections and do something to each element.

Let's look at an example and then see what for loop is all about.

```cpp
#include<iostream>
using namespace std;
int main() {
for (int i = 0; i < 10; i++) {
cout << "hello" << endl;
}
}
```

The output is -

hello

hello

hello

hello

Coding for Beginners

hello

hello

hello

hello

hello

hello

Press any key to continue . . .

The program above basically printed hello ten times. Basically, the for loop that we just defined ran the statement below it 10 times and so "hello" was published ten times.

But why correctly did it run 10 times?

We'll know once we understand the structure of the for loop.

The for loop consists of three parts - initialization, logical comparison, and the increment or decrement statement.

Initialization (int i=0):

In the for loop, the variable i is initialized to the value 0. The variable i works as a counter and at the start of the circle, before any statements are executed, the amount of this variable is 0. That is what initialization means. Also, notice how I didn't have to define the variable outside the loop and then equate it to 0 within the loop (although I can do that as well). The fact that I declared it within the loop means that the variable i will not be accessible outside the loop. However, if I declared it outside the loop and assigned to it an initial value inside the loop, I would still be able to access the variable outside the loop.

Logical Comparison (i<10):

46 | P a g .

The logical comparison defines the condition that needs to be satisfied for the loop to keep executing the statements inside it. This condition is checked every single time the loop is run including the very first iteration. In our example, we check if the variable i is less than 10. If that is true the loop runs, otherwise, the loop is broken.

Increment (or Decrement) (i++):

Every time the loop finishes running, the increment or decrement part is executed. In our example, the value of i increases after every iteration of the loop. But this is also within our control. We could depending on our purposes, decrement the variable we defined or increase it by multiplying it by itself, etc.

How it all works together:

The loop counter is initialized, the condition is checked and if the condition holds, the statement(s) below is/are executed. Then the increment or decrement part is reached and the logical comparison part is rerun. If the condition holds, the loop runs again, if not, it breaks.

The for loop can be used in different ways apart from just as a tool to do something multiple times. We can use it to access elements in our array.

Here's how we can do that -

#include<iostream>

using namespace std;

int main() {

const int arraySize = 10;

int arrayValues[arraySize] = { 1,2,3,4,5,6,7,8,9,10 }; for (int counter = 0; counter < arraySize; counter++) {

cout << arrayValues[counter] << endl;

Coding for Beginners

```
    }
}
```

In the code above, we've first declared the arraySize as 10 and as a constant.

And then we've initialized our array with the numbers from 1-10. Now, instead of individually accessing each element separately, we've used a for loop to do the work for us.

Since the variable counter initially equals 0 and it grows one step at a time and stops at 9, we can use counter's value to index the array's elements at each position.

So, the output would look something like this -

1

2

3

4

5

6

7

8

9

10

Press any key to continue . . .

We can also modify the array's value depending on certain conditions.

```cpp
#include<iostream>

using namespace std;

int main() {

const int arraySize = 10;

 int arrayValues[arraySize] = { 1,2,3,4,5,6,7,8,9,10 }; for (int counter = 0; counter < arraySize; counter++) {

if (counter > 5) {

arrayValues[counter] = arrayValues[counter] * 2;

}

cout << arrayValues[counter] << endl;

}

}
```

In the above program, we've basically written the code such that it would double an array element's value if it's index is greater than 5. The output is as follows -

1

2

3

4

5

6

14

16

Coding for Beginners

18

20

Press any key to continue . . .

Another way to loop is with while loops. Let's explore with an example:

```
#include<iostream>
using namespace std;
int main() {
int arrayValues[5] = { 5,6,7,8,9 };
int counter = 0;
while (counter < 5) {
cout << arrayValues[counter] << endl; counter++;
}
}
```

The while loop executes the statements inside it 5 times in the example. The counter variable is initialized outside the loop and is incremented once all the statements in the loop are specified. If you forget to update the counter, the while loop will run forever!

A slight modification of the while loop above is the **do-while** loop. The do while loop is exactly like the while loop, except that it runs the statements inside at least once, irrespective of the condition.

Let's look at an example based off of the while loops -

```cpp
#include<iostream>

using namespace std;

int main() {

int arrayValues[5] = { 5, 6, 7, 8, 9 }; int counter = 0;

do {

cout << arrayValues[counter] << endl; counter++;

} while (counter < 5);

}
```

In the above program, the statements within the "do" block are run at least once irrespective of the comparison being made. Subsequent iterations are however made on whether the condition is met.

Now that we know quite a bit about loops, let's move back to arrays.

Remember how I said that arrays in C++ are fixed in size? Well, that can't be changed. However, C++ has a built-in container called a vector. A vector is built on top of an array and doesn't have a fixed size. It can be added to as long as you want to.

To use vectors, you have to include the vector library.

As always, let's learn through an example --

```cpp
#include<iostream>

#include<vector>
```

Coding for Beginners

```
using namespace std;
int main() {
vector< int> vec = { 1, 2, 3, 4, 5, 6 }; cout << vec[0] << endl;
vec.push_back(7);
cout << vec[vec.size() - 1] << endl;
}
```

So, you can see that we're using the vector library. And we're initializing the vector "vec" just like we initialized an array. However, there are a couple of differences. The first one is that we're specifying the data type of the vector within angular brackets after the keyword "vector". This data type basically defines the datatype of all the elements within the vector.

Notice how indexing with vectors is just like indexing with arrays.

"vec.push_back(7)" adds the number 7 to vector. So, the vector now contains 1,2,3,4,5,6,7. The ".push_back(7)" notation may be new to you. It basically makes use of the "push_back" method to add a value to the vector. The "." basically specifies that this method applies to the vector you created. We'll look at methods in detail when we talk about Object Oriented Programming.

Just as you added integers to the vector, you can also "pop" integers from the end of the vector. For that you will use the pop_back method - vec.pop_back().

Doing so will remove the last element from the array.

Here is a list of some commonly used vector methods: Method

Purpose

push_back(<value>)

Add's <value> to the end of the vector

pop_back()

Remove the last element from the

vector

insert(<position>,<value>)

Adds <value> to the vector at the

index specified by <index>

clear()

Clears the entire vector

Alright, now let's look at a comprehensive example.

Example - Create a vector containing the scores of all students in a class (the number of students and the scores will be provided by the user).

Calculate the sum of all the scores, and the average score of the class.

```cpp
#include<iostream>
#include<vector>
using namespace std;
int main() {
vector<double> scores;
int numStudents;
```

Coding for Beginners

```cpp
cout << "How many students are in your class?"; cin >> numStudents;

cout << endl << endl;

for (int counter = 1;counter <= numStudents;counter++) {

cout << "Enter the score for student #" << counter << " : ";

double scoreValue;

cin >> scoreValue;

scores.push_back(scoreValue);

}

double classScoreSum = 0;

for (int counter = 0;counter < scores.size();counter++) {

classScoreSum += scores[counter];

}

double average = classScoreSum / numStudents;

cout << endl << "Sum of all the scores - " << classScoreSum << endl; cout << "Class Average - " << average << endl;

}
```

Sample Output:

How many students are in your class? 5

Enter the score for student #1 : 75

Enter the score for student #2 : 70

Enter the score for student #3 : 80

Enter the score for student #4 : 92.75

Enter the score for student #5 : 93.50

Sum of all the scores - 411.25

Class Average - 82.25

Press any key to continue . . .

The first for loop takes in the score for each student and puts the score in a vector. This vector is later accessed and all the scores are added to compute the net score of the class. The average is then calculated by dividing this sum by the number of students in the class.

Example - Build a calculator program that calculates the sum, the product, and the difference between the two numbers and keep doing this until the user enters the string 'STOP'. This program has to run at least once.


```cpp
#include<iostream>

#include<vector>

#include<string>

using namespace std; int main() {

string stopString;
```

Coding for Beginners

```
do {
cout << "Enter the first number: "; double firstNumber;
cin >> firstNumber;
cout << endl << "Enter the second number: "; double secondNumber;
cin >> secondNumber;
cout << endl << "Sum: " << firstNumber + secondNumber << endl; cout << "Product: " << firstNumber*secondNumber << endl; cout << "Difference: " << firstNumber - secondNumber << endl; cout << "Enter STOP if you want to stop otherwise enter any other string";
cin >> stopString;
} while (stopString != "STOP");
}
```

Here's a sample output -

Enter the first number: 1

Enter the second number: 2

Sum: 3

Product: 2

Difference: -1

Enter STOP if you want to stop otherwise enter any other string continue

Enter the first number: 5

Enter the second number: 7

Sum: 12

Product: 35

Difference: -2

Enter STOP if you want to stop otherwise enter any other stringSTOP

Press any key to continue . . .

Coding for Beginners

Chapter 7: Modules

In Python, a module is a portion of a program (an extension file) that can be invoked through other programs without having to write them in every program used.

Besides, they can define classes and variables.

These modules contain related sentences between them and can be used at any time.

The use of the modules is based on using a code (program body, functions, variables) already stored on it called import.

With the use of the modules, it can be observed that Python allows simplifying the programs a lot because it will enable us to simplify the problems into a smaller one to make the code shorter so that programmers do not get lost when looking for something in hundreds of coding lines when making codes.

How to Create a Module?

To create a module in Python, we don't need a lot; it's straightforward.

For example: if you want to create a module that prints a city, we write our code in the editor and save it as "mycity.py".

Once this is done, we will know that this will be the name of our module (omitting the .py sentence), which will be assigned to the global variable __city__.

This is a straightforward code designed for users of Python 2.

The print function is not in parentheses, so that's the way this Python version handles that function.

Coding for Beginners

But, beyond that, we can see that the file "mycity.py" is pretty simple and not complicated at all, since the only thing inside is a function called "print_city" which will have a string as a parameter, and what it will do is to print "Hello, welcome to", and this will concatenate with the string that was entered as a parameter.

Import Statement

This statement is used to import a module.

Through any Python code file, its process is as follows:

- The Python interpreter searches the file system for the current directory where it is executed.

- Then, the interpreter searches for its predefined paths in its configuration.

- When it meets the first match (the name of the module), the interpreter automatically executes it from start to finish.

When importing a module for the first time, Python will generate a compiled .pyc extension file.

This extension file will be used in the following imports of this module.

When the interpreter detects that the module has already been modified since the last time it was generated, it will create a new module.

Example:

This will print:

You must save the imported file in the same directory where Python is using the import statement so that Python can find it.

As we could see in our example, importing a module allows us to improve the functionalities of our program through external files.

Now, let's see some examples. The first one is a calculator where will create a module that performs all the mathematical functions and another program that runs the calculator itself.

The first thing we do is the module "calculator.py" that is responsible for doing all the necessary operations.

Among them are the addition, subtraction, division, and multiplication, as you can see.

We included the use of conditional statements such as if, else, and elif.

We also included the use of exceptions so that the program will not get stuck every time the user enters an erroneous value at the numbers of the calculator for the division.

After that, we will create a program that will have to import the module to so that it manages to do all the pertinent mathematical functions.

At this time, you might be thinking that the only existing modules are the ones that the programmer creates.

The answer is no since Python has modules that come integrated to it.

With them, we will make two more programs: the first one is an improvement of the one that we have just done, and the second one will be an alarm that will print on screen a string periodically.

First example:

The first thing that was done was to create the module, but at first sight, we have a surprise, which is that math was imported.

What does that mean to us?

Well, that we are acquiring the properties of the math module that comes by default in Python.

We see that the calculator function is created that has several options.

Coding for Beginners

If the op value is equal to 1, the addition operation is made.

If it is equal to 2, the subtraction operation is made, and so on.

But so new is from op is equal to 5 because, if this is affirmative, then it will return the value of the square root of the values num1 and num2 through the use of math.sqrt(num1), which returns the result of the root.

Then, if op is equal to 6, using functions "math.radians()" which means that num1 or num2 will become radians since that is the type of value accepted by the functions "math.sin()", meaning that the value of the sin of num1 and num2 will return to us, which will be numbers entered by users arbitrarily who will become radians and then the value of the corresponding sin.

The final thing will be to create the main program, as it can be seen next:

Here, we can see the simple program, since it only imports the module "calculator.py", then the variables num1 and num2 are assigned the value by using an input.

Finally, an operation to do is chosen and to finish is called the calculator function of the calculator module to which we will pass three parameters.

Second example:

We are going to create a module, which has within itself a function that acts as a chronometer in such a way that it returns true in case time ends.

In this module, as you can see, another module is imported, which is called as "time", and as its name refers, functions to operate with times, and has a wide range of functions, from returning dates and times to help to create chronometers, among others.

First, create the cron() function, which starts declaring that the start Alarm variables will be equal to time.time, which means that we are giving an initial value to this function o know the exact moment in which the function was initialized to then enter into an infinite cycle.

Since the restriction is always True, therefore, this cycle will never end, unless the break command is inside it.

Then, within the while cycle, there are several instructions.

The first is that the final variable is equal to time.time() to take into account the specific moment we are located and, therefore to monitor time.

After that, another variable is created called times, and this acquires the value of the final minus start Alarm.

But you will be wondering what the round function does.

It rounds up the values; we do that to work easier.

But this is not enough, therefore, we use an if since, if the subtraction between the end and the beginning is greater or equal to 60, then one minute was completed, and what happens to this?

Why 60?

This is because the time module works with a second and for a minute to elapse, 60 seconds have to be elapsed, therefore, the subtraction between the end and the beginning has to be greater than or equal to 60, in the affirmative case, True will be returned and finally, we will get out of the infinite cycle.

Once the alarm module is finished, we proceed to make the program, as we can see below:

We can see that the program imports two modules, the one we have created, the alarm and the time module.

The first thing we do is to create the variable s as an input which tells the user if he wants to start.

If the answer is affirmative, then the variable h representing the time will be equal to "time.strftime ("%H:%M:%S")", which means that we are using a function of the time module that returns the hour to use in the specified format so that it can then be printed using the print function.

Coding for Beginners

The next action is to use the alarm module using the command alarm.cron(), which means that the cron() function is being called.

When this function is finished, the time will be assigned to the variable h, again, to end printing it and being able to observe its correct operation.

We can say that the modules are fundamental for the proper performance of the programmer since they allow to make the code more legible, in addition, that it enables subdividing the problems to attack them from one to one and thus to carry out the tasks efficiently.

Locate a Module

When importing a module, the interpreter automatically searches the same module for its current address, if this is not available, Python (or its interpreter) will perform a search on the PYTHONPATH environment variable that is nothing more than a list containing directory names with the same syntax as the environment variable.

If, in any particular case, these previous actions failed, Python would look for a default UNIX path (located in /user/local/lib/python on Windows).

The modules are searched in the directory list given by the variable sys.path.

This variable contains the current directory, the PYTHONPATH directory, and the entire directory that comes by default in the installation.

Syntax of PYTHONPATH

A PYTHONPATH syntax made in windows looks like this:

Unlike a PYTHONPATH syntax made in UNIX

Eugene Gates

Coding for Beginners

Chapter 8: Files

Programs are made with input and output in mind.

You input data to the program, the program processes the input, and it ultimately provides you with output.

For example, a calculator will take in numbers and operations you want.

It will then process the operation you wanted.

And then, it will display the result to you as its output.

There are multiple ways for a program to receive input and to produce output.

One of those ways is to read and write data on files.

To start learning how to work with files, you need to learn the open() function.

The open() function has one required parameter and two optional parameters.

The first and required parameter is the file name.

The second parameter is the access mode.

And the third parameter is buffering or buffer size.

The filename parameter requires string data.

The access mode requires string data, but there is a set of string values that you can use and is defaulted to "r".

The buffer size parameter requires an integer and is defaulted to 0.

To practice using the open() function, create a file with the name sampleFile.txt inside your Python directory.

Try this sample code:

Coding for Beginners

```
>>> file1 = open("sampleFile.txt")

>>> _
```

Note that the file function returns a file object.

The statement in the example assigns the file object to variable file1.

The file object has multiple attributes, and three of them are:

- name: This contains the name of the file.

- mode: This includes the access mode you used to access the file.

- closed: This returns False if the file has been opened and True if the file is closed. When you use the open() function, the file is set to open.

Now, access those attributes.

```
>>> file1 = open("sampleFile.txt")

>>> file1.name

'sampleFile.txt'

>>> file1.mode

'r'

>>> file1.closed

False

>>> _
```

Whenever you are finished with a file, close them using the close() method.

```
>>> file1 = open("sampleFile.txt")
```

68 | P a g .

```
>>> file1.closed

False

>>> file1.close()

>>> file1.closed

True

>>> _
```

Remember that closing the file does not delete the variable or object.

To reopen the file, just open and reassign the file object.

For example:

```
>>> file1 = open("sampleFile.txt")

>>> file1.close()

>>> file1 = open(file1.name)

>>> file1.closed

False

>>> _
```

Reading from a File

Before proceeding, open the sampleFile.txt in your text editor.

Type "Hello World" in it and save.

Go back to Python.

To read the contents of the file, use the read() method.

Coding for Beginners

For example:

```
>>> file1 = open("sampleFile.txt")
>>> file1.read()
'Hello World'
>>>
```

File Pointer

Whenever you access a file, Python sets the file pointer.

The file pointer is like your word processor's cursor.

Any operation on the file starts at where the file pointer is.

When you open a file, and when it is set to the default access mode, which is "r" (read-only), the file pointer is set at the beginning of the file.

To know the current position of the file pointer, you can use the tell() method.

For example:

```
>>> file1 = open("sampleFile.txt")
>>> file1.tell()
0
>>>
```

Most of the actions you perform on the file move the file pointer.

For example:

```
>>> file1 = open("sampleFile.txt")
```

```
>>> file1.tell()
0
>>> file1.read()
'Hello World'
>>> file1.tell()
11
>>> file1.read()
''
>>> _
```

To move the file pointer to a position you desire, you can use the seek() function.

For example:

```
>>> file1 = open("sampleFile.txt")
>>> file1.tell()
0
>>> file1.read()
'Hello World'
>>> file1.tell()
11
>>> file1.seek(0)
0
>>> file1.read()
```

Coding for Beginners

'Hello World'

>>> file1.seek(1)

1

>>> file1.read()

'ello World'

>>> _

The seek() method has two parameters. The first is offset, which sets the pointer's position depending on the second parameter.

Also, argument for this parameter is required.

The second parameter is optional.

It is for whence, which dictates where the "seek" will start.

It is set to 0 by default.

- If set to 0, Python will set the pointer's position to the offset argument.

- If set to 1, Python will set the pointer's position relative or in addition to the current position of the pointer.

- If set to 2, Python will set the pointer's position relative or in addition to the file's end.

Note that the last two options require the access mode to have binary access.

If the access mode does not have binary access, the last two options will be useful to determine the current position of the pointer [seek(0, 1)] and the position at the end of the file [seek(0, 2)].

For example:

```
>>> file1 = open("sampleFile.txt")
>>> file1.tell()
0
>>> file1.seek(1)
1
>>> file1.seek(0, 1)
0
>>> file1.seek(0, 2)
11
>>> _
```

File Access Modes

To write to a file, you will need to know more about file access modes in Python.

There are three types of file operations: reading, writing, and appending.

Reading allows you to access and copy any part of the file's content.

Writing allows you to overwrite a file's contents and create a new one.

Appending allows you to write on the file while keeping the other content intact.

There are two types of file access modes: string and binary.

String access allows you to access a file's content as if you are opening a text file.

Binary access allows you to access a file on its rawest form: binary.

In your sample file, accessing it using string access allows you to read the line "Hello World".

Coding for Beginners

Accessing the file using binary access will let you read "Hello World" in binary, which will be b'Hello World'.

For example:

>>> x = open("sampleFile.txt", "rb")

>>> x.read()

b'Hello World'

>>> _

String access is useful for editing text files.

Binary access is useful for anything else, like pictures, compressed files, and executables.

There are multiple values that you can enter in the file access mode parameter of the open() function.

But you do not need to memorize the combination.

You just need to know the letter combinations.

Each letter and symbol stands for an access mode and operation.

For example:

- r = read-only—file pointer placed at the beginning

  o   r+ = read and write

- a = append—file pointer placed at the end

  o   a+ = read and append

- w = overwrite/create—file pointer set to 0 since you create the file

  o   w+ = read and overwrite/create

74 | P a g .

- b = binary

By default, file access mode is set to string.

You need to add b to allow binary access.

For example: "rb".

Writing to a File

When writing to a file, you must always remember that Python overwrites and not insert file.

For example:

```
>>> x = open("sampleFile.txt", "r+")
>>> x.read()
'Hello World'
>>> x.tell(0)
0
>>> x.write("text")
4
>>> x.tell()
4
>>> x.read()
'o World'
>>> x.seek(0)
0
```

Coding for Beginners

```
>>> x.read()
'texto World'
>>> _
```

You might have expected that the resulting text will be "textHello World".

The write method of the file object replaces each character one by one, starting from the current position of the pointer.

Practice Exercise

For practice, you need to perform the following tasks:

- Create a new file named test.txt.

- Write the entire practice exercise instructions on the file.

- Close the file and reopen it.

- Read the file and set the cursor back to 0.

- Close the file and open it using append access mode.

- Add a rewritten version of these instructions at the end of the file.

- Create a new file and put similar content to it by copying the contents of the test.txt file.

Eugene Gates

Chapter 9: Programming Paradigms

What follows is an introduction to the three main programming paradigms based on popularity and application. You've heard me mention when describing different programming languages, whether a specific language was multi-paradigm or not. What this usually means is that with multi-paradigm languages you can code your applications following these three different "styles", even though there are more than just these three. The paradigms are:

- Procedural Programming

- Object-Oriented Programming (OOP)

- Functional Programming

Just like the programming languages themselves, these paradigms came about with the idea to solve specific problems, and then, because we're all lazy monkeys, we ended up forcing them to solve all problems. There is nothing bad about any of them, although you may not believe this from hearing me speak about them. Programming suffers from most of the same issues regular writing does and we can boil them all down to one word: clarity. How to code without repeating yourself? How to organize your code so that you don't end up adding to your workload? How to make sure other people can understand your code? How to make sure you can get back to your code months from now and still understand it? These are all worthy concerns in programming and each paradigm will try to address these problems in their own way.

I chose to introduce the paradigms with the old and tried method of coding the same thing in the three different styles. For this, I decided the game of Cluedo (or Clue depending on where on the globe you grew up in). Not unlike the way we coded the magic tricks, we'll transform a typical game of Cluedo into code. I suspect the choice for this came from the fact that procedural is a word often used to describe a type of murder mystery and because OOP has the idea of "inheritance" as one of its unique concepts and the word put me in mind of rich aunts being murdered for the sake of their millions. I fear my mind thinks in puns.

Coding for Beginners

Be aware that with the exception of the first paradigm, it will feel like you're learning to program all over again. Relax. It's not true. Remember that programming is just a bunch of simple operations (store, add, multiply, compare...) built around strings, numbers, and booleans and abstracted to readable syntax and structures (collections, loops, if statements, and functions). Try to focus on these building blocks first and then take notice of the curious ways things are accomplished through each paradigm. We'll be adding new ways to add context to our code, new kinds of code blocks with their own peculiar rules, and a whole bunch of new syntax and abstractions, but at the heart of it, we're still talking about the same thing.

The paradigms also bleed into each other, the lines between them is quite blurred, and when I introduce a concept connected to one of them I do not mean that concept is not applicable to the others (remember, the languages I've shown you here are all multi-paradigm). You can code procedurally with a slight bent towards objects. You can code objects with a tendency towards functional ideas, and with some functional languages, you can use objects in your logic.

Chapter 10: *Object-Oriented Programming*

Before proceeding, I want you to think about what an object is. Yes, objects that you come across every day. What's common to all objects? The fact that a lot of them have specific characteristics and functions. A pen can have a color and can be used to write. So in the case of a pen, its color is one of its characteristics whereas its function is that it allows people to write with it. Now, this same framework applies to living things too. A dog has a breed, is of a certain height and can bark.

In C++, we can model such objects and work with them. Object-Oriented Programming is basically building a program around objects! Each object has attributes (the characteristics) and methods (the functions/utility). Now in order to create an object, we have to give C++ a blueprint on how to create this specific object that we're trying to make. This blueprint is termed a class. All objects are created from a class and come with a set of attributes and functions that we can use.

Now, a valid question is why? Why do we even need Object Oriented Programming?

The most significant benefit is that it lets us reuse code whenever and wherever we want.

Once I create an object, I can use it wherever I want. And once a class is designed (correctly, without any errors) every purpose that the class produces is free of errors and can be used reliably, therefore, allowing us to create more bug-free code. We don't have to know how an object works once we create it and use it.

We just need to know how to use it. This becomes an advantage when we work with extended programs.

So to recap - An object has functions (we will call these "methods") and attributes (we will call these "instance variables"). There are other types of variables called "static variables" or "class variables".

Objects are created from classes which basically act as blueprints.

Coding for Beginners

```cpp
#include<iostream>
using namespace std;
class EmptyClass {


};
int main() {


EmptyClass emptyClassObject;
}
```

The above program creates an empty class and instantiates an object.

```cpp
class EmptyClass {

};
```

The above stub of code represents the class that we created. Notice how we've used the keyword "class" to specify that we're creating a class. "EmptyClass" is the name of the class we've created. We can change this depending upon the name we wish to give our class. All the instance variables and methods will go within the brackets, but since we created an empty class we don't have any class members.

In the primary function, we've instantiated an object.

```cpp
EmptyClass emptyClassObject;
```

emptyClassObject in the above stub is an object that's created using the EmptyClass class and thus holds all the properties that the class defines. But because we haven't set any properties within EmptyClass, its object is practically useless.

But before we start adding stuff to the class we have to understand what access modifiers are. Now, one of the features of object-oriented programming is that it is able to abstract details of the class from parts of the program outside the class.

This is also known as data hiding. The way we enforce this in C++ is through access modifiers. There are three access modifiers in C++ - private, public, and protected. We're going to look at private and public.

When we use the private access modifier while defining a variable or a method we're basically saying that these members of the class cannot be accessed outside of the class, even by their own objects! These members can only be accessed by methods within the class. If you don't want any part of the code to access certain variables or methods, make them private!

When we use the public access modifier while defining class members, we're saying that they can be accessed from "everywhere". They can be accessed from outside the class using an object of the class.

Example:

#include<iostream>

using namespace std;

class ExampleClass {

private:

int privateVariableOne;

Coding for Beginners

```cpp
public:

int publicVariableOne;

void initializePrivateVariableOne(int value) {

privateVariableOne = value;

}

int incrementPrivateVariableOne() {

privateVariableOne++;

return privateVariableOne;

}

};

int main() {

ExampleClass object;

object.publicVariableOne = 10;

//Error - object.privateVariableOne = 10;

object.initializePrivateVariableOne(20);

//OK! Now, privateVariableOne = 20

object.incrementPrivateVariableOne();

//OK! Now, privateVariableOne = 21

}
```

In ExampleClass, all variables and methods declared under the modifier "private:" are not accessible outside the class. The opposite is true for members declared under the "public:" label which can be accessed outside the class through objects (also called "instances") of the ExampleClass class.

The primary function shows how an instance is created. Akin to how the data type is used while declaring a variable, the name of the class is used while creating an example of the class.

ExampleClass object;

In the above line of code, "object" is an instance of ExampleClass and can access everything that is declared as public within the class. This access is allowed for by using the dot operator (".").

object.publicVariableOne lets us access the publicVariableOne that is tied to the instance. Keep in mind that if we create another example of this class, we'll get access to a completely separate and a brand new example which won't reflect changes made to the first instance that we created - "object" in this case.

Now, there are times when we want to instantiate an object with a set of predefined values. We can do using a constructor, which is declared within the class definition. It has no datatype, and its name is the name of the class followed by brackets that may or may not take in parameters (depending on how you wish to create this class).

Let's add a constructor to ExampleClass:

#include<iostream>

using namespace std;

class ExampleClass {

private:

int privateVariableOne;

public:

Coding for Beginners

```
ExampleClass(int publicVariableValue) {

//This is the constructor

publicVariableOne = publicVariableValue;

}

int publicVariableOne;

void initializePrivateVariableOne(int value) {

privateVariableOne = value;

}

int incrementPrivateVariableOne() {

privateVariableOne++;

return privateVariableOne;

}

};

int main() {

ExampleClass object(30);

//object.publicVariableOne is now 30.

object.publicVariableOne = 10;

//Error - object.privateVariableOne = 10;

object.initializePrivateVariableOne(20);

//OK! Now, privateVariableOne = 20
```

objet.incrementPrivateVariableOne();

//OK! Now, privateVariableOne = 21

}

In the above code stub, the following code represents the constructor -

ExampleClass(int publicVariableValue) {

//This is the constructor

publicVariableOne = publicVariableValue;

}

It takes in an integer and assigns its value to publicVariableOne.

To instantiate an object of the class where the value of publicVariableOne will be 30, we do the following:

ExampleClass object(30);

Now, there's another way of instantiating values in the constructor: ExampleClass(int publicVariableValue):publicVariableOne(publicVariableValue) {

//This is the constructor

}

Example- Create a Dog class that stores a dog's age and the name and has methods called bark and eat.

#include<iostream>

#include<string>

Coding for Beginners

```cpp
using namespace std;
class Dog {
private:
int age;
string name;
public:
Dog(int dogAge, string dogName) :age(dogAge), name(dogName) {}
void printDogName() {
cout << "Dog Name: " << name << endl;
}
void printDogAge() {
cout << "Dog Age: " << age << endl;
}
void bark() {
cout << "WOOOF WOOOOF!!" << endl;
}
void eat() {
cout << "I'm eating right now. Don't bother me!" << endl;
}
};
```

```cpp
int main() {

Dog henryTheDog(2, "Henry");

henryTheDog.printDogName();

henryTheDog.printDogAge();

henryTheDog.bark();

henryTheDog.eat();

}
```

Here's the output -

Dog Name: Henry

Dog Age: 2

WOOOF WOOOOF!!

I'm eating right now. Don't bother me!

Press any key to continue . . .

Coding for Beginners

Chapter 11:   Misconceptions About Coding

Before we dive into this, something should be said about coding. You should not get into it, especially as a career if you don't really like it if it is not something you want to do. Certain people think that being a coder will make you happy, especially when you start earning big bucks. Seriously, more money is not going to make anyone happy. If you're depressed or unhappy, it is something you should find a way to sort out and deal with internally. Visit a therapist, psychologists, do something about it from the inside.

Using coding as a way to escape will only last for so long. Coding is not the way to the proverbial Nirvana or Utopia. Coders also have challenges peculiar to their jobs. Later in this book, we'll talk about some of the challenges coders face. True, being able to make something out of nothing literally comes with some fulfillment, sometimes a lot actually, and it also gives confidence. But if you're looking for happiness, you won't find it in coding or in any other career for that matter. Of course, you won't find it in a person, at least not for long. You are responsible for your own happiness, just as we all are responsible for our happiness. Now that we've got this out of the way let's do a deep dive into misconceptions about coding.

Coding Will Make You Wealthy

Indeed, coders earn good money, and they are some of the top earners in many areas. But then again, the fact that you earn well will not make you rich or wealthy. What will get you wealthier is actually your financial habits; your ability to take the money and then multiply it. You don't have to be a programmer to do this. But then again, being a programmer gives you more room to earn more money, and therefore, more opportunities to become wealthy.

It's only for the Young

They say you can't teach old dogs new tricks, and maybe you can't, but then humans are not dogs. And really, I have always believed that any skill can be learned. You might never become an elite in that skill, but I believe with the right tools and effort, you can become proficient at almost any skill, this includes programming too.

Coding for Beginners

They say it is only for those who are from 18 – 30 years. This could not be further from the truth. It is true that most of the popular coders, or any of those who've really made money from this, started out at an early age: Zuck, Larry Page, Gates, and many others. I just saw on Twitter today, a 45-year-old man who got his first job as a developer, previously having a career in accounting. Admittedly, it would be more difficult to say a middle-aged man or woman to get a junior developer role (entry-level programmer). For some reason, tech firms employ mostly young people. One reason is that most tech firm startups are owned and run by the young, and many older people themselves believe that coding is for the young, so they don't even bother getting into it.

You have To Be a Math Guru to Code

The fact is the amount of math you know at the moment is probably enough for you to learn how to code. At least at entry-level, high school mathematics is good enough for you to begin learning to code. Some people have asked, "What's the connection?" Why do some people think that you have to know mathematics to code? I believe I have the answer to that question. Most universities, which offer computer science or computer science-related degrees, do have a lot of mathematics in their curriculum. In fact, departments of mathematics and statistics in many colleges work hand in hand, and a lot of time, they take the same or similar courses. In some colleges, the departments of math and computer science are together. So you have something department of Mathematics and Computer Science, just like you'd have Mathematics and Statistics in some colleges. This, I think, is how the talk of you being a math guru came up.

For beginner coders, you're just beginning to learn how the Internet and computers really work. You're learning the jargon associated with the field, learning about FTP (file transfer protocols) and debugging, and all the other stuff. Don't forget you have Google, and, as a beginner, virtually all the problems you'll face have been faced by someone else. And the documentation or solutions are somewhere on the World Wide Web. All you need to do is just find it.

Now, this is where your Googling skills will come in. Learning the vocabulary associated with the language you're learning will help you find solutions online easier. At this point, especially when you're teaching yourself, it is a thing of trial and error, Googling, and all through this process, increasing your knowledge. Of course, there's a bit of logic involved in coding. Apart from the little mathematics, you'll actually be doing a lot of copy and pasting, with little edits or tweaks. Although I'd advise, you type in the code instead of copying and pasting. And really you don't need any mathematics to do this. In fact, those who came from fields where no Mathematics was needed, such as those in humanities, seem to know how to do this well. Remember the term papers.

Some codes look like equations true, but then there are plug-ins and add-ons for such things. Some people live for such things, and most of the time, these calculations have already been taken care of in one way or the other, and all you'll need to do it tweak it for your own use. So for web development, you don't need much of mathematics. But if you intend to go into video gaming, or you want to work in some high tech places like Google, Goldman Sachs, NASA, then yes, you'll need to know mathematics, loads and loads of it. For those doing AI, Crypto and other related fields, some of the math needed is even above college undergrad level, yeah it's that essential.

So what I'm basically trying to say is that for entry-level coding, don't bother about mathematics, because you already have enough knowledge for that. As you delve deeper, though, you'll realize the knowledge you don't have or need and do whatever it takes to get there. But by this time, you should already know enough coding to work in a variety of places where coding is required.

The fact is that there are not many programmers that really known mathematics, so knowing it will give you an edge, especially when it comes to getting a job. But as a beginner or someone who will build CMS (content management systems), you know all the math that you need.

Programming is Only for Geeks and Nerdy Fellows

The fact is that programming doesn't make you a geek. You're a nerd if you are, and you're not; if you're not, it has nothing to do with programming. People also think that programming is for the uncool gang, you know the social misfits, the socially inept and awkward. Now, nothing could be further from the truth than this. Coding doesn't turn you into any of this, nor is it only for those who have some sort of social problem. Coding is also done by some of those we'd

Coding for Beginners

consider cool. Coding is now seeing use in clubs, wherewith code you can decide the kind of music to be played. Or you can even write music with code, for clubs and other fun places.

Programming is Only for Men

Of recent, certain companies such as Andela have entirely changed that notion, with the training and employment of female coders. Programming is not gender-based; anybody, irrespective of gender, can do it. The reason why we have many more males in coding than women is the reason why we have more men in engineering and science and related fields. Men seem to be naturally drawn toward STEM, while more women seem to gravitate towards the humanities, art, and fashion. And of course, the self-limiting belief and talks of people always telling women they can't succeed in STEM-based fields. But we know all these things are wrong. Coding is gender-neutral, given the same opportunities; women can code as good as men can. And did you know that the first programmer was actually a woman? Her name was Ada Lovelace, Countess of Lovelace, a British Mathematician and writer. She was born in 1815, and she died 36 years later. In fact, at about that time, most of the programming work was done by women. It was as an offshoot of their secretarial duties. As time went along, though, things changed.

To Be a Programmer, You need a Degree in Computer Science

Or the very least, a degree in STEM. This is one very big lie that a lot of people have been sold, by who? Really I can't tell. Perhaps some 15- 20 years ago, a higher institution was the only place where you could get learn coding. And then you had to have taken a degree in computer science. But now every Tom, Dick, and Harry can learn how to program. In a university, it will definitely take you longer to learn how to code, and of course, there'll be students debts to be paid. However, it will definitely give you a good learning platform and better preparation to learn many other programming languages and also give you better career opportunities in tech. However, it is not the only way. Just online with Freecodecamp, Coursera, or Udemy and uncountable others, you can learn how to code at your own pace. There are also coding boot camps, where you can learn how to code and meet other students like you. The fact is that you'll just need to be persistent, know what you want, and create a schedule for yourself to follow.

With this, you'll learn code in like a quarter of the time it will take someone following a university curriculum to learn how to code.

Coding for Beginners

Chapter 12:   Bash

Given the following Bash Code:

```
#!/bin/sh
cat 'testfile.txt' |
while read line ; do
  echo "Line read: $line"
  outputDirectory=${line##* }
  echo "Output directory: $outputDirectory"
  mv $outputDirectory/streamFolder/output/*.log
$outputDirectory/streamFolder/output/archive/ > /dev/null 2>&1
  mv $outputDirectory/streamFolder/output/*.txt
$outputDirectory/streamFolder/output/archive/ > /dev/null 2>&1
done
```

Let's now apply the coding metrics to the above Bash script. Here is the list of metrics.

1. Too short variable names and has no usage context

2. Code that gives no context or obvious purpose

3. Uneven spacing

4. Uneven parameter type definition

5. Incomprehensible code

6. Too long code

7. No exemption handling

8. No automatic resource management

9. External calls that are not kept in separate methods

Coding for Beginners

10. Insufficient abstraction - need for higher level code

11. Code that is hard or impossible to change

Out of the metrics, I think only a few apply in the case of this Bash code. This is an important issue: In real world code, don't expect it to be all bad! If you're modifying legacy code, the original author may well have done a great job with it. If this is the case, then your task is more straightforward.

In this case, the required change may be straightforward. However, there may also arise a situation where you can make an improvement as part of another change. We'll see this in the present example.

So, in my opinion the Bash code violates metrics 7 and 10 only:

- No exception handling

- Inadequate abstraction - need for higher level code

Why is this the case? Well, the calls to mv can fail and we won't know about it. This is because the script is coded to swallow output and errors. How do I know this? The clue is in the redirect code: > /dev/null 2>&1. This has the intentional effect of not letting us see the result of the preceding mv operation.

So, as per metric 7, we need to at least record if an exception occurs in the calls to mv.

In regard to inadequate abstraction, the file name can be made into a constant. Then, the constant can be referenced in the script. This is better than embedding the name as a literal string value, mainly if the file name is used in multiple places in the script. A downstream maintainer might be tasked with changing the script and could easily forget to change the file name in all areas. Defining the file name as a constant avoids this unpleasant possibility.

So, with all of the above observations in mind, Listing 1 is the modified version of the Bash code.

Eugene Gates

Listing 1 Post-metric Bash code

```sh
#!/bin/sh
readonly fileName='testfile.txt'

cat $fileName |
while read line ; do
  echo "Line read: $line"
  outputDirectory=${line##* }
  echo "Output directory: $outputDirectory"
  mv $outputDirectory/streamFolder/output/*.log
$outputDirectory/streamFolder/output/archive/ > /dev/null 2>&1
  error=$?
  if [ $error -ne 0 ] ; then
    echo "First mv failed with exit code of $error"
  fi
  mv $outputDirectory/streamFolder/output/*.txt
$outputDirectory/streamFolder/output/archive/ > /dev/null 2>&1
  error=$?
  if [ $error -ne 0 ] ; then
    echo "Second mv failed with exit code of $error"
  fi
done
```

Notice in Listing 1 that we now have a constant called fileName representing the file name. This constant can now be used throughout the script instead of embedding the file name. So, if a different file name is required at some future time, then it has to be changed in just one place instead of potentially multiple places in the script.

The other major change is to store and examine the error code from each of the mv calls. This allows us to know for sure if the mv call succeeded or not. To complete the example, it

Coding for Beginners

would probably make sense to log the error code details to disk. But, you get the idea! Following the metrics helps to take the guesswork out of the code, mainly when errors occur.

There is still an issue with inadequate abstraction (metric 10) in Listing 1. Can you see it? The new error handling code is an improvement, but it has introduced a problem with code duplication. We should really try to fix this, and one way to do this is to abstract the error handling code itself into a function. Listing 2 illustrates the final offering for the Bash code.

Listing 2 Second iteration of the post-metric Bash code

```sh
#!/bin/sh

readonly fileName='testfile.txt'
errorHandler() {
  echo $1
  echo $2
  if [ $2 -ne 0 ] ; then
    echo "Failed in errorHandler $1 Exit code is $2"
  fi
}

cat $fileName |
while read line ; do
  echo "Line read: $line"
  outputDirectory=${line##* }
  echo "Output directory: $outputDirectory"
  mv $outputDirectory/streamFolder/output/*.log
$outputDirectory/streamFolder/output/archive/ > /dev/null 2>&1
  errorHandler "first call to mv", $?
  mv $outputDirectory/streamFolder/output/*.txt
```

98 | P a g .

```
$outputDirectory/streamFolder/output/archive/ > /dev/null 2>&1
  errorHandler "second call to mv", $?
done
```

Now, any failures that occur during execution of the code in Listing 2 appear as illustrated in Listing 3. These errors can be logged to disk if required by adding more code to the errorHandler function.

Listing 3 - Running the modified Bash code

```
Line read: mydirectory
Output directory: mydirectory
first call to mv,
1
Failed in errorHandler first call to mv, Exit code is 1
second call to mv,
1
Failed in errorHandler second call to mv, Exit code is 1
```

Notice also, that by following the metrics the script in Listing 2 is nicely divided (or modularized) into three parts:

1. Definition of constants

2. Definition of error handler and other functions

3. The main code

Also noteworthy in this example was the fact that we iterated twice through the metrics. Again, this is a good practice - making small, focused changes, reviewing the changes, and adding more minor changes. The combination of the small changes adds up to a far better end result and the code can be tested carefully as you go.

One noteworthy caveat is in relation to spacing. There might be a temptation on the part of a Java (or other high level language) programmer to introduce spaces into Listing 2. This might

Coding for Beginners

be done to try to improve readability. One of the things about scripting languages, such as, Bash and Python is that they are often very fussy about spaces, indentation, and so on. Adding spaces to Bash code can introduce hard to find errors. So, be careful with readability requirements!

Up to this point, we've seen the metrics in action in C code and now in Bash scripting. How can the metrics approach be applied to Python code? Let's find out.

A Python example

Given the following Python code.

```
f=open('myfile','r+')
f.write('abcdef012345')
```

As usual, let's apply the metrics to the Python code. Again, here is the list of metrics.

1. Too short variable names and has no usage context

2. Code that provides no context or obvious purpose

3. Uneven spacing

4. Uneven parameter type definition

5. Incomprehensible code

6. Code that is too long

7. No exemption handling

8. No automatic resource management

9. External calls that are not contained in separate methods

10. Inadequate abstraction - need for higher level code

11. Code that is difficult or impossible to change

I would say that the following metrics are violated by the Python code:

- Variable names that are too short and provide no usage context

- Inconsistent spacing

- No exception handling

- No automatic resource management

- External calls that are not contained in separate methods

Also, we have some assumptions lying at the heart of the Python code example.

What are the assumptions? Well, the first line assumes that the file already exists and the second line in turn assumes that the first line was successful.

A simpler and sturdier version is illustrated in Listing 4 where we use the standard exception management of the Python language. Also, I've tried to improve the file handle name by giving it some context in the wider program.

Listing 4 - Incorporating better naming and exception management

```
try:
  logfile = open('myfile', 'r+')
  logfile.write('abcdef012345')
except IOError:
  print('Encountered an error')
```

Now if the file is deleted before the script runs, then you get a meaningful message rather than a runtime failure. It's essential always to remember that when your code interacts with system resources (such as files), you're handling somebody else's property! System resources are owned by the system, so you have to handle them with care.

The moral of the story is to keep it simple and try to avoid assumptions. Mother nature enjoys assumptions; they give her an opportunity to show us who's boss!

Coding for Beginners

The addition of exception code has still not produced particularly reliable operation. We are still relying on the file existing in order for the code to work. To fix this, before opening the file, we can first check that it exists as illustrated in Listing 5:

Listing 5 - Incorporating an existence check

```
try:
  if(os.path.isfile('myfile')):
    logfile = open('myfile', 'r+')
    logfile.write('abcdef012345')
  else:
    print('File does not exist')
except IOError:
  print('Encountered an error')
```

So, the code now uses isfile() to check if the file exists before attempting to open and update it. This means that we have now removed the assumption about the file existence. If the file does not exist, then we'll know upfront, rather than relying on an exception.

Chapter 13:   ***Regular Expressions***

The Simple Patterns

The simple patterns are direct literal representations of the anticipated inputs. First we present the necessary characters for the formation of simple regular expression patterns.

Simple Pattern Characters

Characters	Functions
/.../	Patterns are enclosed in between two forward slashes like this /a/. This matches a single alphabetic letter 'a' in an input string "ant".
[...]	The braces represent a character set. The character set matches any of the characters within the braces with no exceptions for special characters and escape sequences, for example [abc] would match the first three letters of the input string "abcdef". A range can be represented with a hyphen like this [1-9], which matches any character from 1 to 9, same as [123456789].
\	When the backslash character precedes a character, it makes the character unique and gives it a special meaning different from its literal meaning.
\d	The lower case letter 'd' preceded by a backslash represents a numerical input and matches a single digit, for example /\d/ matches digit 3 in the input string "32 Highway".

Coding for Beginners

\D	The upper case letter 'D' preceded by a backslash represents any non numerical input and matches a single non digit input, for example /\D/ matches 'H' in "32 Highway".
\w	The lower case letter 'w' proceeded by the backslash character represents a single alphanumeric character in the range 0 - 9, a – z, A – Z including the underscore.
\W	The upper case letter 'W' preceded by the backslash character represents a non alphanumeric character like the followings; @, %, * and so on for example /\W/ matches the '@' in the email address feyi_dos1@yahoo.com.

The Simple Pattern Quantifier

Pattern quantifiers are used for specifying the frequency of occurrence of the affected character under representation by the regular expression. The quantifiers are presented in the table below.

Quantifiers	Function
?	This when applied to regular expression character implies 0 or 1 occurrence of that character. This can also be replaced with {0, 1}. For example the proper expression /Shoes?/ or /Shoes{0,1}/ matches the string "Shoe" in "Shoe lace".
*	The quantifier '*' implies zero or more occurrence of the regular expression character under representation. It can be replaced with {0,}. For example the regular expression /lo*/ or /lo{0,}/ would match the character 'l' in string "lives" and the sub-string "loo" in the string "looses"

104 | P a g

+	The quantifier '+' implies one or more occurrence of the regular expression character under representation. The quantifier can also be replaced with {1,}. For example the regular expression /lo+/ or /lo{1,}/ would find no match in the string "life" but would find the match "loo" in the string "looses".

The Simple Patterns Formulation

We proceed to the implementation phase of the simple regular expression patterns, starting with the development of an HTML5 input form. It will validate the user inputs with JavaScript using our designed regular expression patterns. We begin with the noun class pattern.

The Noun Class Patterns

The noun class represents the name of a person, a place or a concept on an input form. This can be one of the following input fields; place of birth, religion, nationality, occupation and name.

A name is made up of alphabetic characters with the characters in upper or lower cases. To represent this, we use the following simple regular expression; a combination of simple characters and quantifiers as shown below.

Step 1:

We create the regular expression pattern for the first letters which normally should be a single capital letter and in some exceptional cases can be more than one. We use the character set A to Z to represent the pattern as shown below:

Coding for Beginners

[A-Z]+

Remember the quantifier '+' implies one or more occurrence of the upper case character set A to Z. We need this representation to be followed by lower case character set a to z. The lower case character set is represented as follows:

[a–z]+

Now we want a combination of the two sets, to achieve this we combine the two sets as shown below.

[A-Z]+[a-zA-Z]+

Meaning you can have a noun class written in upper cases all through and a noun class starting with an uppercase character, followed with a combination of high and lowercases. In summary a noun class must begin with a capital letter. The quantifiers ensure there is at least an alphabetical input for both the upper and lower cases.

The Complex Patterns

The complex patterns are the combinations of simple characters, complex characters, the alphanumeric, the non-alphabetic characters and the quantifiers. We start off with the complex characters.

Complex characters	Functions

$	Matches a character occupying the last position in the input string, for example /r$/ matches the last alphabetic character 'r' in the input string "reader", but finds no match in the input string "read" or "READER" for the match is case sensitive.
^	Matches a character occupying the first position in the input string. For example /^e/ matches 'e' in the string "eat".
.	Represents a single character input and matches the character input. For example the regular expression /.n/ matches the letters 'In' in the string "Into" and /.o/ matches the letters "to" in the string "to".
A|B	The '|' special character also called the 'OR' operator matches A or B, whichever it finds in the input string. For example the regular expression /boy|girl/ matches 'boy' in the input string "boy scout", girl in the input string "girl scout" and girl in the input string "girl or boy" whichever it finds first.
\s	Represents and matches a white space character, a tab or a form feed.
\S	Represents and matches a non-space character.
(…)	The capturing parentheses match their contents as single entities and also remember the match for future usage. \1 to \n denotes the sequence number of the parenthesized matched items to be remembered. For example, the regular expression /\w+(\s)\d+\1\w+/ matches the string "No 42 Highway" in the input string "No 42 Highway road". The only capturing parenthesis is remembered with '\1' in the expression and applied as a white space between "42" and "Highway".

Coding for Beginners

(?:a)	The expression (?:a) represents a set of non capturing parentheses that match but do not remember the match as done by the capturing parentheses. The main purpose of the non capturing parentheses is for creating sub expressions to be matched in a regular expression. For example in the expression /(\w)+\s(?:\d+)\s\1/ the numeric part (?:\d) is matched but never remembered.
A(?=B)	This acts like a look ahead. It matches the expression A provided that it is immediately followed by an expression B. For example the regular expression /Coca(?=Cola)/ matches "Coca" if and only if it is followed by "Cola" and it is case sensitive. The regular expression /No(?=\d+)/ matches "No" if and only if it is followed by one or more numbers.
A(?!B)	The regular expression matches an expression A provided it is not followed by an expression B. For example the regular expression /No(?!\W)/ would match nothing in the strings "No%" and "No@" but would match the "No" in the string "No1 Gateway".
[^abc]	This expression represents a complimented character set that matches any character set not in the complimented set. A range can be represented with a dash. For example the regular expression [^abc] performs the same function as the regular expression [^a-c] and matches the character 'r' in the string "car".

A Username Expression Implementation

The username is a combination of alphanumeric characters beginning with at least an alphabetic character. There are two steps to this.

Step 1:

The alphabetic character is represented with the regular expression /[a-zA-Z]/ which matches any single upper or lower case alphabetic input. We expect that our username should start with a minimum of a single alphabetical input, for this reason we make use of the quantifier "+" to arrive at the following expression:

/[a-zA-Z]+/

Step 2:

We also expect that the above may be followed by a combination of alphanumeric characters. The regular expression /\w/ gives a good fit. The quantifier "*" (zero or more times) is used with the expression for a complete representation as shown below:

/\w*/

Step 3:

The final step is to combine the alphabetic regular expression with the alphanumeric regular expression such that the alphabetic is matched if followed by an alphanumeric expression or not. This is as presented below:

/[a-zA-Z]+\w*/

Complex Regular Expression Implementation

Coding for Beginners

Examples of complex patterns are the email address and dates. We shall be formulating the email address as a follow up practise to our username implementation. An email address is has two parts; the username part and the server address part separated by the '@' sign. Therefore the formulation process is divided into two stages.

Stage 1: Username Formulation

This is as done in 2.2 above..

Stage 2: Server Address Formulation

The sever address will always start with the '@' symbol. This can be represented literally by the '@ symbol itself followed by the organization's name, which can be represented by a username expression as shown below:

/@[a-zA-Z]+\w*/

This is followed by the organization's categorization (.com, .mil, .net, .org, .edu) preceded by a full stop .e.g. yahoo.com as implemented below:

/(\.)[A–Za-z]{2,3}/

Note that the categorization is written in a minimum of two alphabetic characters and a maximum of three, the reason for the use of the quantifier {2,3} and that the expression for the full stop '\.' Is enclosed in a capturing parenthesis in order for it to be matched and remembered for a later re-use. This may be followed by the country name as in .us, .uk, or .ng. As observed this uses a maximum of two letters so that it can be represented with the following regular expression:

110 | P a g

/(\.)[A–Za-z]{2}/

The quantifier {2} accepts two character length input only. Now bringing the components together we have the regular expression:

/@[a-zA-Z]+\w*(\.)[A–Za-z]{2,3}(?:\1[A–Za-z]{2})*/

The above regular expression would match the server name "@yahoo.com" in the input string "123@yahoo.common". Please note that the country code component which is enclosed in a non-capturing parenthesis '(?:\1[A–Za-z]{2})*' has been made optional with the use of the quantifier '*'.

Step 3: Combining the Username and the Domain name

The final step is to combine the username and the domain name regular expression to arrive at the complete pattern for matching an email address as shown below:

/[a-zA-Z]+\w*(?:@)[a-zA-Z]+\w*(\.)[A–Za-z]{2,3}(?:\1[A–Za-z]{2})*/

From here on, you can design and implement any desired pattern for any particular validation purpose, all you need is a little more practise though. Remember, practise makes perfection. I wish you success in your practise.

Coding for Beginners

Chapter 14: Data Structures

List

Explanation: A list represents a set of ordered elements, which means that each component can have another element before or after it. A linked list consist of **nodes** that contain **data**. Each node, or position **gets** a certain ordering number, depending on its ordering in the list: we talk about the first element, the second etc. Each node **contains** a value; it can be an integer, a string etc. When we refer to a specific position (for example when we talk about the first element), there is maximum one entry that may satisfy our request. This means that we cannot have two or more elements in a position.

The first node is called **head**. Internally, each node points to the **next** one, and the last one points to **null**. In Python we do not have to worry about pointers.

Implementation: We can name our list with a name of our liking, usually something that represents its functionality (be careful not to use a built-in python name!).

Lets name our list **a**.

In the brackets that follow the name of our list, we place the index, the position which we refer to:

a[0] refers to the element at the **first** position (**position 0**). We need to assign a value in this cell.

a[0] = 5, assigns 5 in the **first** node of our list.

So, we have:

list[index] = value

We can easily create a list in Python. In order to define a list (initially empty) we just do:

Coding for Beginners

a = []

Else, we could initialize our list with some data:

b = [2,5,4]

Note that we do not have to specify the positions of our elements each time, as the first element will always be in position 0 (b[0] is 2), the second in position 1 (b[1] is 5) etc.

We can add add an element x in the end of the list:

list.append(x)

For example, b.append(7) will give us:

b = [2,5,4,7]

We can also add an element x in a certain position I of the list.

list.insert(i,x)

For example in our previous list, we can do b.insert(0,3), which will give us:

b = [3,2,5,4,7]

We can remove an element that contains a certain value:

list.remove(x)

Note that this will delete the first element that contains this certain value.

For example in our previous list, if we do b.remove(2), we will get:

b = [3,5,4,7]

Tuple

Explanation: Tuples serve a similar functionality with lists, with the main difference being that tuples are immutable: as soon as you add your data in a tuple, they cannot be changed or deleted and it is not possible to insert new data. The only way to perform such operations is to create a new tuple containing the new or edited data etc.

In terms of syntax, tuples use parentheses to store the data in place of the lists' square brackets. There is also the possibility not to include parentheses at all, and just separate data with a comma.

When we need to refer to a certain position in the tuple, for example position 0 (first element), position 1 (second element) etc, square brackets are used.

Implementation: We can create an empty tuple named t:

t = ()

We can also create a tuple that contains some numbers:

t_2 = (9,4,6,8,2)

or:

t_2 = 9,4,6,8,2

Now, we can refer to a certain element of the tuple, like for example the first element:

t_2[0] = 9

Dictionary

Explanation: A dictionary is used to store data by using a unique key for each entry. Key is somehow serving the same functionality as indices in lists and tuples, when we want to refer to a certain element. The values where each key refers to are not necessarily unique. Dictionaries are mutable, so we can add, delete or modify the elements in it.

Coding for Beginners

The entries of a dictionary are contained between curly braces {}. Each entry is in the form key: value.

Implementation: We have a dictionary d:

d = {}

and we can populate it with key-value pairs:

d = { key1:value1,

key2:value2,

key3:value3,

...

}

Set

Explanation: A set is a collection of items that in contrast to lists/tuples, it is unordered. There can be no duplicate elements. Sets are efficient when we want to search if an item is contained in them or not. Later on, we are going to talk about hash functions, which implement efficient searching. We can add, delete or modify the items in a set. The set items are contained in {}.

Implementation: We can define an empty set s_empty:

s_empty = {}

or we can construct a set of certain items, like a set of fruits:

s_fruits = {'orange', 'banana', 'apple', 'peach'}

We can add an item using the add() function:

s_fruits.add('cherry')

'cherry' will be added in a random position in the initial set (remember, sets are unordered!). For example:

s_fruits = {'orange', 'banana', 'cherry','apple', 'peach'}

or we can add multiple items in the s_fruits set using the update() function:

s_fruits.update(['grapes', 'mango'])

s_fruits = {'orange', 'grapes', 'banana', 'cherry','apple', 'peach', 'mango'}

Array

Explanation: An array consists of an ordered collection of elements. We can refer to each item by its index in the array. An array can have dimensions: the widely used 2-dimensional table that we encounter very often in our everyday life, but we can also have more dimensions. In computer science theory, the difference between an array and a list is the way data are stored in memory, which affects how we access an element. A list allocates non sequential cells in memory, therefore they need a reference for the next cell; this is what the index does. Lists support sequential access, where you need to search an element by examining the first element, then the next one, afterwards the third one etc until you find the element you are looking for. An array allocates only sequential cells in memory. Arrays support sequential access, as well as direct access.

Implementation: You may have noticed that Python lists have some array-like features, according to the list analysis above. Python in fact uses array functionalities in lists, like for example direct access to a certain position. However, there is an array structure in Python, but it should be imported:

Coding for Beginners

import array

We need to specify the data type that this array contains and also the list of elements that the array is going to contain when we are creating it. For example:

a = array.array('i', [1,2,3])

Yes, array keyword is written twice, because we are calling the array module from the array library. It is easier to rename the imported library array though:

import array as arr

a = arr.array('i', [1,2,3])

'i' refers to int Python type. Below is the list of all supported Python data types and the letter they use to indicate this data type when we construct an array:

Code	C Type	Python Type	Min bytes
'b'	signed char	int	1
'B'	unsigned char	int	1
'u'	Py_UNICODE	Unicode	2
'h'	signed short	int	2
'H'	unsigned short	int	2
'i'	signed int	int	2
'I'	unsigned int	int	2
'l'	signed long	int	4
'L'	unsigned long	int	4
'f'	float	float	4
'd'	double	float	8

Stack

Explanation: Stack is used to store items in the Last in – First out (LIFO) manner. Operations like insert element (push) and remove element (pop) can occur only from the 'upper' end of the stack. An overflow can occur if we exceed the maximum size of the stack, while an underflow can occur if we try to delete an element from an empty stack.

Implementation: In Python a stack can be implemented by using a list structure. We can create a simple stack:

stack = []

Pop elements from the stack

stack.pop()# '3'

stack.pop()# '2'

stack.pop() # '1'

Queue

Explanation: A queue handles item in the first in – first out (FIFO) manner. We can add (enqueue) items from the 'end' of the queue and delete (dequeue) items from the 'beginning' of the queue. Overflow and underflow can occur as in the case of the stack.

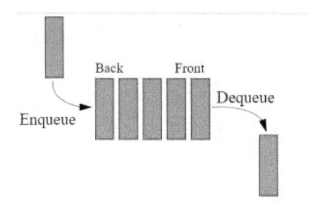

Implementation: In Python we can import the queue module:

import queue

Then we can create a queue by calling the method Queue in that module. We can add (put) elements and we can delete (get) them in the FIFO way:

q = queue.Queue(maxsize = 100)

q.put('a')

q.put('b')

q.put('c')

q = ['a','b','c']

q.get()# 'a'

q.get()# 'b'

q.get()# 'c'

Graph

A graph is a representation of a set of objects (nodes or vertices V) where some of them are connected with links (edges **E**). Formally, a graph G is defined as pairs (V, E) .

We can dynamically add and remove vertices and edges.

Note that the above is an undirected graph: this means that the connections between the vertices have no direction, for example ab = ba etc.

In case of directed graphs there are directed arrows ⟶ as edges, and we can move only towards the direction of the arrow.

A sequence of edges that connect a vertex with another, either directly or indirectly, forms a path. \

Tree

Trees are a subtype of graphs, which needs to satisfy the following requirements:

- It needs to be acyclic: to contain no cycles

- It needs to be connected: Any node should be reachable through some path, so there are not 'stray' nodes

Coding for Beginners

Typically, the tree has a structure of a root node and children nodes. Root node can be only one and it can have any number of children nodes (directly connected to the root nodes). Any child can have any number of children etc. Nodes that do not have children are called leaves.

Chapter 15:   *Algorithms*

Algorithm

I n the coding phase, all the modules defined by the modular design will become a program; that is, the final application will consist of the sum of all the programs that are designed. But first, we must determine what the instructions or actions of each of these programs are. To do this, algorithms must be used.

An algorithm establishes, in a generic and informal way, the sequence of steps or actions that solves a certain problem. The algorithms constitute the main documentation that is needed to be able to start the coding phase, and, to represent them, two types of notation are essentially used: pseudocode and flowcharts. The design of an algorithm is independent of the language that will later be used to encode it.

Pseudocode

The pseudocode is an algorithmic programming language; It is an intermediate language between natural language and any specific programming language, such as C, FORTRAN, Pascal, etc. There is no formal or standard pseudocode notation, but each programmer can use their own.

An algorithm written in pseudocode is usually organized in three sections: header, declarations, and body. In the header section, the name of the algorithm is written, in this case, add. In the declarations section, some of the objects that the program will use are declared. In the tutorial of the language of Abrirllave, the different types of objects that can be used in a program are studied in detail, such as variables, constants, subprograms, etc. For now, note that, in this example, the variables a, b, and c, they indicate that the program needs three spaces in the main

Coding for Beginners

memory of the computer to store three integers. Each of the variables refers to a different memory space.

Flowcharts (Ordinograms)

Algorithms can also be represented, graphically, by means of flowcharts. Flowcharts can be used for other purposes; however, in this tutorial, we will only use them to represent algorithms. Such flow charts are also known as audiograms. In other words, an ordinogram graphically represents the order of the steps or actions of an algorithm.

Pseudocode and flowcharts are the two most used tools to design algorithms in structured programming. Although, between both types of representation, there are the following important differences:

Flowcharts Began To Be Used Before the Pseudocode

In pseudocode, three sections of the algorithm are usually defined (header, declarations, and body). However, in one ordinogram only the body is represented.

In an ordinogram it is usually easier to see, at first glance, what the order of the algorithm's actions is.

The graphic symbols used in a flowchart have been standardized by the American National Standards Institute (ANSI). However, there is no "standard pseudocode."

Qualities of an algorithm

For any given problem there is no single algorithmic solution; It is the task of the person who designs an algorithm to find the most optimal solution, this is none other than one that more faithfully meets the desirable qualities of any well-designed algorithm:

- Finitude. An algorithm always has to end after a finite number of actions. When the Add algorithm is already a program, its execution will always be the same, since, the actions described in the body of the algorithm will always be followed, one by one, from the first to the last and in the established order.

- Accuracy. All the actions of an algorithm must be well defined, that is, no action can be ambiguous, but each one of them must only be interpreted in a unique way. In other words, if the program resulting from an algorithm is executed several times with the same input data, in all cases, the same output data will be obtained.

- Clarity. Normally, a problem can be solved in different ways. Therefore, one of the most important tasks of the designer of an algorithm is to find the most readable solution, that is, the most understandable for the human being.

- Generality. An algorithm must solve general problems. For example, the Add program should be used to make sums of any two whole numbers, and not only to add two specific numbers, such as 3 and 5.

- Efficiency. The execution of the program resulting from coding an algorithm should consume as little as possible the available resources of the computer (memory, CPU time, etc.).

- Simplicity. Sometimes, finding the most efficient algorithmic solution to a problem can lead to writing a very complex algorithm, affecting its clarity. Therefore, we must try to make the solution simple, even at the cost of losing a bit of efficiency, that is, we must find a balance between clarity and efficiency. Writing simple, clear, and efficient algorithms is achieved based on practice.

- Modularity. Never forget the fact that an algorithm can be part of the solution to a bigger problem. But, in turn, this algorithm must be broken down into others, as long as this favors its clarity.

The person who designs an algorithm must be aware that all the properties of an algorithm will be transmitted to the resulting program.

Chapter 16:   *Logical Switches*

Logical Switches are very similar to a series of if statements, in that they allow for many different conditions to be checked and have varied output depending on the value we are checking against. They look cleaner than a series of 'if' statements, and there is some additional functionality that can be done with switches that sometimes makes the desirable. Let's look at a basic switch now.

switch (variable) {

case condition1:

// some code based on what you're doing

break;// exits the switch loop

case condition2:

// more code for what happens for this condition

break;

case condition3:

// you can have as many cases as you like

break;

default;

// code to do if none of the other cases are true

In this example, we can see the format that switches take. The term 'variable' is a component you will use to measure some varying quantity in your sketch. The conditions, one, two, three, as many as you like, are values you are comparing a variable against. They can be anything, numbers, letters, words, even other variables, or the results of functions it is kind of crazy what

Coding for Beginners

you can put as a condition. This is why they can be extremely powerful in coding. You can make complex conditions or simple ones, and both will have a clean, readable layout that has a very easy to understand flow when you read it. This readability in your code is so important for us humans to understand what is going on with it.

The code within each case will continue until it reaches the word 'break' which is an Arduino keyword and this tells the compiler that it should exit the current function it is doing. In the case of a switch, it will exit the switch when a break is encountered. If a break is missing from the code, it will instead continue on and run the next line of code below in the next case, which may leave unexpected results. It's best to make sure you add break to your code at the same time as a case to make sure the code you're writing will flow properly.

Let's look at an example sketch:

> File → Examples → 05.Control → switchCase

Okay, we start off with initializing our sensor minimum and maximums in the form of constants that the coder determined from experiment. In setup() we turn on serial communication so we can use our serial display. In the loop function, we declare and initialize the variable we will use to read our sensor, sensorReading. Zero to Six Hundred is a lot of cases to cover if we just want to display relative brightness of the display. The user wanted four data points to generalize the brightness, ranging from zero to four. They, therefore, used the map() function, along with sensorReading, sensorMin, sensorMax, 0, and 3 as the arguments, to scale the reading should be within a 0-3 range instead. Notably, the map function will scale to the nearest integer so we can safely know it will only contain four data points.

We now set up a switch to check the reading. We send 'range' to our mapped sensor reading and have the switch as our variable. Our cases are 0, 1, 2, 3, which corresponds to the expected data range of our variable, good so far. Now, if range got mapped to 0, we will print, dark. If range gets mapped to 1, we will print dim. For range 2, medium, and for range 3, bright. The user added a 1-millisecond delay for stability, forcing it to read once per millisecond instead of

128 | P a g

much faster. Essentially the chip clock speed, which by default, is 16Mhz or sixteen million instructions per second.

Let's take a look at another switch example. Open up:

File → Examples → 05.Control → switchCase2

In this next example, again we see and initialize 'Serial' communications like we've done before. Then we initialize our pins to OUTPUT using a 'for' loop, cycling from pins two through seven by one each pass. Next, we have to check if we have received a character input from the serial port (greater than zero means not FALSE), we will then create an integer which will read the input from our keyboard. Alphanumeric keys come in the form of ASCII characters, so for example 'a' = 97, 'b' = 98, 'c' = 99, etc. This is why we record the input as an integer from Serial.read().

Next, we reach our switch, which varies based on the value we recorded from our keyboard input inByte. We have set five possible cases and a default in case we get a character other than our case values. For any character a, b, c, d, e, we will toggle an LED to high. For any other value, we will sequentially turn the LEDs off going from lowest to highest, using a 'for' loop.

This example shows that you can base your cases off of almost any kind of variable. It doesn't have to be an integer. They can be anything you feel you need to check what is happening in your sketch and react to that condition.

Switches are a fantastic way to keep your code elegant and organized.

Coding for Beginners

Chapter 17: Coding Practices

Contained in this will be some of the best practices you can adapt to take your coding to a higher standard. We have touched on this first topic already, but we will expand and reiterate here. First up is naming conventions.

Here are some best practices for your comments that will help other readers understand you easier:

- Start with a summary of the sketch and what it will accomplish. Provide any links if it helps the understanding of your design. Try to approach your block comments from a user-friendly stance as much as possible to give a clear idea of what you will be doing.

- Write in the active voice. Use a clear, conversational tone for your writing, as if you were speaking to another person standing next to you.

- For instructions to the user, use the second person, to invoke in the user that they should be the ones to carry out your instructions.

- Use short descriptive phrases rather than complex phrases. It is easier to understand one simple idea at a time.

- Be explicit about what you are doing with your actions. For example: "Next, you'll read the value of the sensor on pin thisPin."

- Avoid phrases or words that are 'fluff' or do not contribute to the explanation, e.g. you see, you'd want to, etc. Instead, skip those words and give a statement that's direct to the point, e.g. set the pins.

- Check your assumptions, make sure you have explained all of your ideas and haven't left something that can only be explained 'in your head.'

Coding for Beginners

- Give a description for every variable or constant with a comment of its purpose either before, or in line with the variable or constant.

- Similarly, give an explanation of a block of code that you're about to perform before the instructions are executed, so it's clear what's about to happen.

- Every loop should have comments explaining why this loop exists (e.g. what it is doing), and a verbal explanation of its condition if it's still not clear.

Coding Best Practices

- Follow naming conventions

Do not create one letter variable names! Your naming conventions exist so that you can, at a glance, read your code without having to refer to other places to understand what is going on.

- Write code that is reusable or modular

User-defined functions are a great way to accomplish this. By doing this, you can write a segment of code in just one place and refer to it each time it is necessary. This makes better sense and is much cleaner and simpler to read.

- Write a flow-chart of your sketch before you start coding

Seriously, this cannot be overstated how valuable this step is to write clean code. By knowing all the pieces you will need to accomplish your sketch's task ahead of time conceptually, you can successfully plan ahead and use things like functions in a smart way.

- Keep things organize and together

If you make a function to smooth an analog sensor, make sure that's all it does. Don't start doing other parts of your code within that function. If your function needs to, you can have it call yet another function to help it accomplish its task. Again think modular (small pieces make a big part).

- Make yourself a toolbox

Make functions that do specific things. Then use your tools as needed in your code.

- Keep your sketches

Even if you think you won't need a sketch you made anymore, keep them. If you need a piece of code that you've already written for another project and you have followed these practices, you can simply snag that piece of code and drop it into the new project you're working on. Brilliant!

- Write your functions in a generalized way whenever possible for these exact reasons

To put this simply, it means that if you were making a function to draw a square, make a function to draw a rectangle instead since a square is a special case of a rectangle, where the edges are equal.

- Make sure your functions do what they say they will do

E.g., if it is a function named 'flickerLeds' (pinValue), it better be flickering some LEDs!

- Avoid pointers

We didn't even touch on them in this document, and we are only going to tell you they exist to tell you not to use them unless you're an advanced user. They are the most likely 'tool' to cause the crazy, bad kinds of problems from happening in your coding, and are notoriously tough for a beginner to use properly. So avoid them until you are sure you know what you are doing.

- Embrace self-improvement

Understand from day 1 that as a fledgling coder that you will grow and improve over time. Use each challenge you come across to try writing new sketches as an opportunity to grow and hone your skills.

- Reach out to the community for help and advice!

Coding for Beginners

There are some really fantastic people in our big community of hobbyists that are willing to help you learn and grow as an enthusiast.

- Try to make things foolproof when you code

Try to make sure your for loops terminate, try to account for unexpected inputs when checking values, try to constrain your data within expected values. These 'tedious' steps are what keeps your program running smooth and bug-free!

- Know how to use debugging tools and techniques

It's a more advanced topic but learning about debugging tools and techniques for large-scale projects such as robotics, or as a controller for something like a pump mechanism will help expand your knowledge further.

- Write both brackets or both braces at the start then fill in the date in-between

When writing functions, loops or anything with brackets and braces, this trick helps to ensure that you will be closing all of your brackets and braces, preventing unexpected results.

- Try new ways to use your Arduino!

This is how you can really develop new skills. When you have more skills, you can think of even more things you can do with the chip! The possibilities with this micro-controller are nearly limitless and are bound only by the limits of your imagination.

More Naming Best Practices

- Functions follow the same rules as variables

The name should start with a lower-case letter, all one word, and additional words are distinguished with capital letters.

- Functions should use verb names to describe their function

E.g. stepMotor(), getValue(), smoothReadings(), etc. All these names explain with an action word what this function should be doing.

- Make the name describe the purpose of the function

- Make sure the for loop variables are clear on what they represent

Having a variable of x can work, but it really offers nothing to the person reading your code for them to understand exactly what that variable is for.

Coding for Beginners

Chapter 18: How to Be an Expert Coder in the Shortest Time Possible

Coding is not the easiest thing to do; at least this is something almost everyone new to coding will agree with. However, as you actually go on, you'd discover that coding is actually not so hard, challenging, yes, and it will actually always remain challenging, but difficult and almost impossible, that is just at the beginning. You'll also discover that what you might find infinitely difficult might just be learning your first language. This is quite understandable as you're just getting into a new field. As you learn more languages, you'll discover that it actually becomes easier. The previous languages just seem to prepare you to learn a newer one, irrespective of the language that you've learned. This, I guess, is the reason lots of coders advise that you learn HTML first. Although it's not a programming language, it is very easy to learn and put into practice, and it has a way of preparing yours for more difficult language in no time.

So how does one become an expert coder in the shortest possible time? In fact, who's an expert coder, and how long will it take before someone can be regarded as that?

The fact is that if you ask 5 different people in tech, they'll give you five different answers about who an expert coder is. Here's the way I'd define an expert coder. I consider an expert coder as one who can write good code. Anyone can actually learn how to write code; writing good code, though, is a different thing entirely. And this is where the tough part is, I think it should be the aspiration of every coder to be able to write, neat, good, free-flowing code.

Refuse To Be Intimidated

This is usually the first problem that beguiles most people learning code for the first time. Especially those who think it is for the mathematical geniuses. It all starts in your mind; you have to rid yourself of any form of intimidation. "Anything can be learned," never forget this phrase. I'm not trying to excite you up like a motivational speaker, though I'm not saying this is bad in any way, I'm just trying to present the facts before you. And with the array of resources

Coding for Beginners

available on coding, you'd be able to find a class or two that totally resonates with your learning pattern.

Learn How To Learn

This, for me, is the most important skill every developer needs. Irrespective of how far you've gone into coding, or how little about coding that you know. Learn how to effectively learn, because you'd continue learning as long as you're a coder. There's no point in the life of a programmer when he can really say I have arrived, I have learned all that needs to be learned. This character is something I have found amongst musicians, both professional and those who do it as a hobby. When we meet at events and someone does an introduction, which goes thus, "meet my badass keyboardist friend," and then the badass keyboardist will say something along these lines "please pay him no mind, I'm just a learner." And as the introductions go round, and someone introduces someone who he thinks is an excellent musician, the instrumentalist friend says, "I'm still learning." At the event, a lot of times, it would turn out that a lot of the guys are actually excellent instrument players. At first, I thought it was fake humility until I started learning to play the keyboard. And the better I got, the more I realized that there was so much more to learn about playing the instrument.

This is something most programmers understand; there's always something to be learned. There are new code bases, new challenges you encounter as you tackle novel projects, both personal and at work.

The rate at which the tech world is changing is astronomical. There are new updates to languages, new tools and frameworks, and many other new features coming out every day. A developer needs to be able to keep up; otherwise, he/she will be left behind.

Learning is not easy. If it were, well, we'd have knowledgeable people around us every day. If you really want to learn how to learn, then I'd suggest that you take coursera's course. The course title is "Learning How to Learn: Powerful mental tools to help you master tough subjects." At this point, you'd agree that learning to code is a tough subject. The course is free, and you'd be able to apply the skills and techniques you learn there to any form of learning in your life, both technical and non-technical. This is like the best free course I have taken all year, and I recommend it to everyone who needs to or wants to keep on learning. It's going to make your learning more efficient. I'll also suggest that you read Cal Newport's book "Deep Work." The book contains strategies on how to learn faster and also be more productive. It also has a very inspiring story about some guy learning how to code and becoming very good at it and getting well paid. I don't remember the fellow's name, but the thing is that this guy was an entry-level accountant, but he wanted more, so he taught himself how to code. And all these happened in less than a year.

As far as learning code is concerned, there'll be no point where you might be able to say; I have learned it all; therefore, I know it all. Learning for a coder is a continuous process; it never ends, the challenges, the pressure to be the best you can be, it will not end. Perhaps until you decide to stop coding, but one thing though that it that learning coding will get easier as you go along. The better you get, the easier and faster it becomes for you to learn more coding related things.

Learn To Write Code; Try the Hands-on Approach

There is the temptation by certain persons wanting to learn code to read all the materials they can get on the language, read blog posts, and watch videos before even writing a line for code. For effective learning, I'll say you should begin writing code as soon as possible. That's another reason I suggest you start learning from HTML; you can see the results of your code immediately. You might think that you've gotten the concept of how to code a certain feature because you saw the documentation, or you read it in a book only to want to try it out, and you're stumped. This, I think, is one reason I love freecodecamp, each concept you learn is paired with a relevant exercise so that you can try out your hand on a concept. Until then, no matter how much you think that you understood the concept from the lesson until you do something with it, you can't be so sure. Something else with coding is that things don't usually work right the first time; you'd be stumped many times. So it's better you get used to getting stumped and learning also to get yourself out of the quagmire.

Coding for Beginners

Another way to reinforce learning faster is to use coding games, challenges, and other interactive tutorials to reinforce learning. Hour of Code is one coding game you might want to give a try, CodinGame is another coding game you might want to try, it is more complex, but also you might be able to put it on your resume.

Learn Computational Skills

Computational thinking is very important for a programmer. This is where you learn to solve problems in the way a computer can interpret. These skills are what people acquire when they study computer science. So you see, a computer science degree is not a waste after all. Some of the topics you'll encounter include loops, algorithms, recognizing patterns, amongst others. These concepts will equip you with the skills to understand programming languages easier and faster. With this knowledge, too, you can take on more difficult projects and even design better products. Ideally, the place you'll get this knowledge is from a degree program in computer science from a university. However, there are online resources where you can learn computer science for free or a token price. EdX, Coursera and MIT OpenCourseware are some of the places you can learn about computer science. You can also get videos on this YouTube channel.

Projects

You really can't say that you've understood a language well until you've used it in a project. In fact, if you don't have projects in a certain language, you might not be able to prove in a job interview that you really understood a certain language. A project tasks you on most or all of the knowledge you have acquired in a certain language. It reinforces what you've learned, and also it pushes you to learn more. See, you don't have to wait until you've gotten to the end of the course before you start attempting projects. Some platforms like freecode camp have projects, real-life projects for real-life organizations which you can tackle as a way to challenge yourself.

If you're looking to get into coding things very fast, you should start coding with a project in mind, even without knowing jack about the language. It is one easy way to learn about the features and tools. So you might decide that you want to learn Android development, and then with your skills, you want to be able to build an alarm clock app for your phone. So you go online to search for resources on how to make that happen. In the process of learning to build an alarm clock, you'll definitely learn a lot. It's a more difficult route to use in learning, but it is a very effective one.

Tinker with Other Peoples' Code

This is after you've grasped the basics of whatever language you're learning. At this point, it is time to find someone else's code, play around with it, and see what happens. There are places where you can find code files; one of them is GitHub. Open the file in your code editor and get to work. Try to read the lines of code and try to see if you can understand what each line does. If you can improve it, so if you have questions about the code, ask, if you have comments, make them. And if, for any reason, you improved on the code, upload it to GitHub or any developer forum you're on and see people's feedback.

Join Developer Forums

This goes without saying. Development is not done in isolation. It's a group of people building on what others have built and improving what others have created. Most developers are open-hearted as far as sharing coding knowledge is concerned. On these platforms, you can get people to answer your questions, give you advice, share knowledge, and even get mentored. Slack Overflow is a good place to be as someone learning to code. You'd be inspired; you'd be challenged and encouraged by what you see in these forums.

Coding for Beginners

Chapter 19:   *Other Factors*

Becoming the best programmers depends on many factors besides learning programming techniques in classes or over the internet. In simple terms, it is not about programming as most beginners think. From my experience, your level of impacts plays a lot in determining the level of your success or how best you are as a programmer. Truly, people will not measure your experience from how happy you look when doing programing projects but how your programming projects are impacting the lives of many people in society. For example, there are some people who always feel happy after spending the whole day without doing any programming tasks while others feel unhappy if they do not handle any projects. Also, drinking alcohol everyday can make a person feel happy. Therefore, your level of experience and knowledge does not show how happy you are but how you use the learned skills.

Several studies have proved that slacking off in computer programming not only makes person's programming logic weaker but also destroys his/her tempo. Normally, we miss many things when we don't attend the classes just like drinking coke every day ruins both our teeth and internal organs. Just like alcohol has impacts in our bodies, your success in programming is measured through its impacts. We will see you as a weaker programmer if you do not use the learned programming skills to create positive impact to you or to the society.

Levels of Impacts Resulting From Programming

Ideally, there are different levels of impacts we can use to determine how perfect you are with programming. Yes, most programmers do not know that their programming knowledge is judged on how it impacts them or the society. The following are levels of the impacts:

First Level of Impact: You/ A Person

Coding for Beginners

One of the step to determine how you can measure the impact is by looking at the effects of programming has made on an individual. It is not only the simplest way but also very important since all programmers have goals in their mind before starting programming. Usually, you engage in various activities or jobs because you want a result not nothing. For example, we take our children to schools with two reasons; (1) get job in their future lives to live better life, and (2) obtain knowledge that will help them associate with other people in the society. It is important to know that doing something without a purpose makes you to experience an unexpected result on your way. Therefore, the impacts of programming on you show how best and successful you are as a programmer.

Relationships in Life

Do you know that programming can cause certain impacts on your relationship? In order to determine the effects of programming on your relationship, we always look at how close you are to your love, friends, and other people in the society. Some people chose to be software programmers because it is their passion while others chose it because their friends are doing it or their parents forced them.

Another main reason why people chose programming is getting jobs. In most cases, we work in projects, deliver them, and earn income once users use them. As programmers, we are only required to maintain the projects if there are crashes or bugs. This gives us more time to spend on our relationships. Truly, human life is all about relationship but not how much we earn per day. You may be earning five or six digits but you are not happy at all because you lack freedom to associate with people, particularly your love ones and relatives. Let me tell you, people get more fulfillments out of life when there are some people whom they love and care for. You should spend your earnings with the people you love. As such, work is supposed to improve your relationship with love and relatives.

Impacts on Your Health and Life

In this modern life, your mind and body are the two main assets you must value most. Both body and mind are irreplaceable in our life. Therefore, you must take care of our mind and bodies to avoid them deteriorating over the time. Surely, every person wants to have a longer life, and as such, it is important to consider health when measuring how best you are as a programmer. You career as a programmer would not be either good if you are not healthy.

Money is worthless when compared to our mind and health. I tell you, money will always come on your way when you develop a good mind, which include practicing daily to solve problems, looking for answers, and thinking deep and creatively. You should not only get enough sleep but also build a habit that will train your mind just like writing and reading books. Make coding to be a favorite way to train you. The best programmers always spend at least thirty to forty minutes per day on programming. This is very important to their health. We can say health is your life and you should take care of it in order to live longer.

Having Full Enjoyment

We have seen previously that happy is not the measurement of the success of a person; it is only a part of it, though we need it. You can increase your productivity in programming by engaging in things that you enjoy. What do I mean? I mean that a person can be more productivity in his/her programming work if he/she gives himself/herself a chance to enjoy life. Being more productivity in programming has more impact too. In addition, you should know that there is a great difference between passion and hobbies. While hobby refers to doing something you enjoy, passion refers to thing you like doing throughout the life. For example, my passion is coding and my hobby is learning Japanese language. I always study Japanese when I am a little bit frustrated with some complex coding. This gives enough time to refresh my mind before diving back into the world of coding.

It is always better to give yourself enough time to relax or take a break to make your brain work on the problem subconsciously. But what do you do if you find it hard to solve the problem even after relaxing? It is easy. Just give your brain enough time to solve the problem in the

Coding for Beginners

background. In fact, this is one of the main reasons why most ideas come in our minds when we are eating, showering, or drinking tea.

The Second Level of Impact:

This is to know how your programming knowledge and skills impact other people and the society at large.

Impact on Others

Before you consider yourself as the best programmers, it is important to ask yourself about the impact you cause to other people when you are coding. Okay, you may be like that you know how to code because it is the most useful tool available for impacting the lives of many people positively. You can impact people by either enabling them to get data easily, improve their websites, or increase sales. Every person must have a goal in mind why you are doing a particular job. One of the goals in programming is helping other people achieve their objectives. You will be recognized as the best programmers when you help others and organizations to succeed and at the same time meeting your goals. I know it is sometimes difficult for most programmers, but you can become the best programmers if you do this.

Giving Purpose to Other People

Every person has a purpose in life, and this is seen when an individual dedicate his/her life to doing certain thing. For programmers, their purpose is revealed when they engage in building projects and software. Now, let us ask ourselves where this sense of purpose comes from. In normal cases, our purpose comes from the surrounding, society, friends, and internet. For example, we develop an interest in programming after we encounter those who do programming and have achieved a lot in their lives. To be precise, they are the main people who

146 | P a g

can inspire you to engage in programming. But what will you do in case those people fail to give us ideas? There is a higher chance that you will not have a right purpose. We all have different purpose in our lives and that is the main reason why we all do different work. We were not born to do the same job. While some people are born to be developers, others are born to be doctors, teachers, or politicians.

According to Mark Zuckerberg during his Harvard Commencement Speech, people must have a generational challenge for our society to continue moving forward. We should not only create new jobs for the youth or our people but promote a sense of purpose. However, it is not easy to have a purpose for yourself. You should also create a sense of purpose to other people in the society. Let us take the following example. You need to hire workers if you build a company. These workers play a significant role to the growth of your company. It is, however, your responsibility, as an employer, not only to give them a sense of purpose but also help them to grow in society.

Coding for Beginners

Chapter 20:   *Landing a Job*

Getting A Job Without Experience

Getting started with finding your first job can be difficult. There is quite a bit of competition. Many recent college graduates compete for the same position as you.

 How to be chosen from all the other candidates?

The answer is to differentiate yourself, stand out from the rest.

What is the type of job you want?

The first thing you should do to stand out from the rest and get your first job even if you don't have experience is to know what you want.

Do you want to be a front end developer, a back end developer or a mobile developer? Neither is better than the other, it is about what you like, you will spend the following years of your life coding, what better it is in those technologies that you love.

Study the market offers

You have already decided the type of developer you will be, now you must know what you need to know or know to get the desired job.

Depending on the country where you live, there are Internet portals where employers publish the available job offers. Perform a search, you can try for example with "Developer backend jr". Do not be in a hurry to apply for whatever job that appears in your search. What you should do is analyze the market.

Coding for Beginners

Most of the job offers will ask you for technologies that you must know and divide them into two sections,

Required which you must know to get the job and the desired ones that are a plus or extra if you know them.

Analyze various job offers and analyze the technologies that are repeated and make a list of them. It will serve you later.

Some job offers publish the salary range and the benefits they offer in others wait to make a call if they are interested in your profile. I'm going to tell you this to give you an idea of what you can earn in your first job, since getting out of that rank can affect your chances of being hired.

Acquire the skills you need for your dream job

Here is a news that will be a bit harsh. Everything you learned in college during your 4 or 5 years spent in it is not enough for the world of work.

Most of what you learned just lays the groundwork for what's next (in addition to giving you that valuable piece of paper called a title that companies still ask to employ you).

Do you remember the list you made with the desired and required technologies that are most repeated to you according to your choice of type of development you want to dedicate yourself to? It is time to use it.

You will have to study and master these technologies. Most companies will give you an oral or written exam to verify that you can perform the job for which they are hiring you. So study and strive.

You can choose to review free tutorials on the Internet or videos on YouTube. But my recommendation is that you buy courses on Udemy or Platzi since their teachers and community will answer your questions and guide you step by step. This will save you a lot of time, unlike searching for information scattered throughout the Internet.

Show your knowledge

Now how do you show the employer that you have the necessary knowledge?

Having no experience, you must demonstrate in another way that you have the ability you claim to have.

In programming there is nothing better than github to demonstrate your skills.

If you do not know Git and Github you are one step behind your competition, but do not worry it is not something that with a little study you cannot remedy.

Show off your skills by writing a blog or YouTube. Do not expect to fill the blog with advertising or become a youtuber. The objective is not that. The objective is to demonstrate that you have the necessary knowledge.

You want to go one step further, buy a domain with your name and a hosting. It will make you look more professional.

The last option to demonstrate your knowledge is certifications. Certifications are documents issued by authorized companies that when you pass an exam (quite difficult at times) certify that you have extensive knowledge of this technology.

Create a linkedIn account, fill out your profile to be visible and have an online presence make sure to link your github or website.

Creating a Perfect Resume

Coding for Beginners

Forget about putting the information of your preschool and high school, just put relevant information, and put the information of your university only. You can also put information about your middle school if it has technical training in computer science or similar if it is not, also omit it.

The information you fill out will be related to your acquired skills.

Write all the technologies in which you have knowledge and link to the blog, YouTube channel, Github or website where you demonstrate it.

Never you to put technologies that you do not know in your CV, it will automatically untie you from the selection process and if it is very easy to notice it in a technical interview, believe me.

Postulant

It's time to go back to the Job Search Portals and fill them with your information, your new knowledge and your online github profiles and personal sites.

Do a search with the characteristics you want from the job.

In the course you will find dubious offers, it is better to avoid them since they will slow down your development.

I don't know if you noticed it during your search, but it is in the big cities that most of the offers are concentrated in addition to being the best paid. If you live in one of them you will have no problems, but if not, sooner or later you will have to move.

In your search you have already found several companies where you would like to work, contact them and send that resume that you made with so much effort and patiently waiting for an answer. You can do this once a day with new offers.

Eugene Gates

Coding for Beginners

Conclusion

The best way to learn programming is really just to challenge yourself. Start putting yourself out there and seeking programming challenges. Think of something that you want to do and then start looking into whether other people have done it. If they have, look into the way that they did it and try to find a way that you could do it yourself. If they haven't, then this gives you a perfect opportunity to be the first to do something. Get your hands dirty and start looking into and learning as much about things having to do with programming as you possibly can.

I'm going to say this right now: Programming is not easy. You have a long and arduous journey ahead of you, and the truth about programming is that to be a programmer means to submit yourself to constantly learning. At no point in programming do you ever consider yourself "done with learning'.

One of the big problems they face when starting in this programming world is that when you start you want to make complex programs, pages, and professional applications, but at the critical moment there can be some difficulties, even when you have the experience, for this reason, we decided to share some tips to shorten the learning curve:

1-Know the origins first.

This does not mean that you completely learn the history of the computer, but you must know it, that will give you the notion of how everything came about, so you will know how everything works, from data to an operating system.

2-Master basic concepts.

Know computer concepts such as what is a data, record, field, information among others. As theoretical and boring as this may seem, it will help a future to understand how multiple functions work and why they are made that way.

3- Make an algorithm before starting to throw codes.

Coding for Beginners

If you do not know what it is sincerely I tell you that you will less understand what you do, this is a serious mistake that many programmers make that we do not give importance to the analysis before starting, I advise you that if you are starting as a programmer, you first practice informal algorithms, then it happens to the computations.

This will open up your logic as a programmer and will make a kind of connection between your mind and the computer so that both friends can easily understand.

4-Study fundamental functions of programming

When we start as a programmer, it is necessary that we know perfectly the functions like for "for," while "while," if "if" but "else," among others, where our code starts, because it must have an end and a set of fundamental operations that are in general use.

And you will ask yourself: What is all this for me to learn any programming language? Simple and straightforward programming in general, and in any programming language be it Python, PHP, C ++, C, C #, Java, etc. a "for" will remain a "for" an "if" will continue to be "if" and a "function" will continue to be "function" the only thing that varies are the details of the language's own syntax.

5-Anyone can program

You must trust yourself and be persevering, what makes good programmers is not that they have exceptional talent better than everyone or anything like that, rather they know and master the concepts that I have mentioned before, This means that they are made to learn both a new language and to understand well what they do as programmers.

Be patient read, study, use the documentation that is offered, one of my teachers says that when he started as a programmer he made many mistakes, and it was very difficult to adapt to programming, today he is one of the best and most recognized programmers from my country.

If you take these tips to the letter, success as a programmer awaits you, and many doors will open in this wonderful world of technology.

Coding for Beginners

CPSIA information can be obtained
at www.ICGtesting.com
Printed in the USA
LVHW102241190921
698227LV00020B/407